THOSE WHO HEARD IT FIRST:

*The Political Implications of the Sermon on the Mount
to Jesus' Jewish audience*

A Thesis by Roger E. Lang

Learn more about
Dr. Jen Betham-Lang and
Roger Lang's ministry at:

www.bnai-tikkun.org.nz

LANG Book Publishing Ltd.

Cover design by Blair McLean.

ISBN-13:

    978-0-9941117-2-2 – Paperback

    978-0-9941117-3-9 – eBook (Kindle)

Published in New Zealand

DEDICATION

This publication is dedicated first and foremost to HaShem who is the source of all inspiration for us all. May all those who read this dissertation find knowledge and the joy of G-d.

Thank you to Jennifer Betham-Lang who is my partner and source of life and joy and a continual source of thoughts and prayers. You are a great inspiration. Thank you to my children Paul, Immanuel, and Jemma who in their laughs spawn creativity and inspiration. May God always guide you.

Thank you to Dulcie who is a wonderful support and pillar to lean on and for always being supportive of all that I do.

Thank you to Blair for having the creativity to make everything look beautiful and making a great cover design.

CONTENTS

CHAPTER I

INTRODUCTION

There is much in Christianity that is unique but also many elements of similarity with other religious and ethical traditions. In particular, there is significant continuity with Judaism. An accurate depiction of the Christian religion requires that the novelty of Christianity should be neither overstated nor underestimated. The element of Christianity central to this dissertation is the peace sayings of the Sermon on the Mount, the whole of which can be seen as the essence of Jesus' ethical and religious teachings. The political implications of those ethical and religious teachings have been the topic of prolonged and earnest debate within Christianity since its inception. The political stances adopted by the followers of Jesus over the last two thousand years have varied immensely from pacifism (a rejection of violence) and political passivism (a rejection of political engagement) to an active and armed support of the political system, be it the Roman Empire, medieval feudalism, or modern states.

The focus of this dissertation departs from the popular Christian interpretations of the political implications of the Sermon on the Mount. Instead, it examines the original Jewish intellectual context of the Sermon and its likely Jewish reception. It seeks to outline the Jewish framework through which Jesus' first audience would have interpreted those political implications. It is beyond the scope of this dissertation to establish what Jesus "meant" or the political implications he favoured. Jesus wrote nothing. We have only the records of others as to what he said. The sermon exists in two forms in the canonical Bible - in the Gospels of Matthew and Luke. We do not know whether the Sermon was delivered as a unified oration or whether it is a compilation of utterances from different times in Jesus' life. Either way, those who heard first what Jesus said were predominantly Jewish.

The content of the Sermon on the Mount is similar to other sayings found in both Judaism and Christianity. According to Hill, "religions are distinguished less by their unparalleled elements than by the way common elements are shaped and assembled."[1] For example, biblical scholarship has found that Genesis 1-11 shares numerous features with other ancient Near Eastern creation stories, but the theological contours of these chapters are singular and significant.[2] According to Geza Vermes, biblical scholarship has found that Jesus' Sermon on the Mount and the peace sayings within it have much in common with Jewish religious and political thought around the time of Jesus.[3] This is something agreed on both by 'conservative' evangelical biblical scholars such as Keener and Hagner and by 'mainline' scholars such as Davies and Allison. Regardless of perspective, scholarly commentaries on Matthew's Gospel and the Sermon on the Mount now cite numerous parallels to Jewish and rabbinic literature to help interpret Jesus' teaching – the most extensive being Keener, and Davies and Allison.[4]

This dissertation contributes to that scholarship by furthering understanding of the contemporary Jewish context of Jesus' teaching about peace, violence and resistance. It outlines the important parts of the Jewish intellectual framework from within which Jesus' first audience would have interpreted the political implications of the Sermon on the Mount and its peace sayings. Furthermore, it establishes the likely meaning of Jesus' Sermon on the Mount and its peace sayings in terms of Jewish understandings of his time.

---

[1] Craig C. Hill, *In God's Time: The Bible and the Future* (Grand Rapids, MI: Eerdmans, 2002), 40.

[2] John H. Walton, *The Lost World of Genesis One: Ancient Cosmology and the Origins of Debate* (Downers Grove, IL: InterVarsity Press, 2009); Gordon J. Wenham, *Genesis 1-15*. vol. 1a, Word Biblical Commentary (Waco, Texas: Word Books, 1987), 40.

[3] Geza Vermes, *The Religion of Jesus the Jew* (London: SCM Press, 1993), 30.

[4] Davies and Allison, *Matthew 1-7*; Keener, *Gospel of Matthew*.

1.1 **The Research Question**

We do not know exactly what Jesus said—we have only second-hand accounts of his sayings in translation (primarily the four canonical gospels). We do not know precisely what Jesus meant—that has been hotly debated for almost two thousand years. This dissertation investigates not what Jesus meant, but what his audience heard and were likely to have understood. It does this in order to ascertain the novelty or otherwise of Jesus' teachings with regard to Jewish thought and political understandings of his time. His audience was primarily Jewish, and the political implications they drew from Jesus' teachings would have been influenced by established Jewish thought on ethics and governance. This dissertation researches specifically this: how would Jesus' Jewish listeners have interpreted the peace sayings of the Sermon on the Mount?

1.1.1 Objective of Research

The objective of this research is to set out the Jewish intellectual context of Jesus' preaching. It aims to portray accurately the ethical and religious thought of Jewish people at the time of Jesus. By doing so, the novelty and continuity of Jesus' teachings can be established.

1.1.2 Type of Research

This research is descriptive rather than analytic. It describes the state of Jewish thought on ethics and politics at the time of Jesus. It is fundamental rather than applied – knowledge is gathered to understand better the intellectual context of Jesus' teaching, rather than to solve a problem. It is historical in that it uses documents and texts from the past to study the religio-political philosophy of the Jewish people in the first century CE. The research is qualitative rather than quantitative–it investigates subjective attitudes, interpretations, and impressions.

1.1.3 Methodology

The research method is literary: namely, the analysis and description of historical Jewish writings in order to establish the politico-ethical frameworks of the time.

1.1.4 Dating of Matthew

The dating of Matthew's account of the Sermon is important to this dissertation as it sets the end-date for the Jewish writings that influenced this gospel writer. By 33 CE, Jesus had been crucified. The accounts of the Sermon on the Mount appear in the gospel of Matthew and in the gospel of Luke; however, the focus will be on the gospel of Matthew because of the stronger Jewish intent found in the writing. There is much debate over its date. The majority of scholarly opinion places its date after 80 CE.[5] A minority of academic thought places the writing of Matthew later; Carson and Moo date the book around 100 CE, and Meier dates Matthew around to 85 CE.[6,7]

The author of Matthew may have used various sources to compile the document.[8] It is now widely accepted that it was written after Mark: "Given some time for Mark to circulate and to be read, and given some time for a dispute with a local Antiochene synagogue to develop after the crisis of 70 CE, a date for Matthew in the 80s is likely."[9] The prominent Jewish scholar, Jacob Neusner, suggests that the date of the book is 80 CE.[10] The religious

---

[5] Dale C. Allison, *The Sermon on the Mount* (New York: Crossroad, 1999), 96; Warren Carter, *Matthew and Empire* (Harrisburg, PA: Trinity International, 2001), 37; Jacob Neusner and Bruce Chilton, *Judaism in the New Testament* (London: Routledge, 1950), 118.

[6] D. A. Carson and Douglas J. Moo, *An Introduction to the New Testament* (Grand Rapids, MI: Zondervan, 2005), 152.

[7] John P. Meier, *A Marginal Jew.* vol. 4 (London: Yale University Press, 2009), 42.

[8] Robert J. Miller, *The Complete Gospels* (Santa Rosa, CA: Polebridge, 1992), 54.

[9] Warren Carter, *Matthew and Empire* (Harrisburg, PA: Trinity International, 2001), 37.

[10] Neusner and Chilton, *Judaism in the New Testament,* 118.

orientation of the writer is a matter of debate too. Sigal highlights the extent to which the beliefs of the writer are questioned:

> W. D. Davies and Reinhart Hummel argued that the redactor of Matthew was a Christian Jew. Krister Stendahl's view was that Matthew was a redactor of a work that took shape in a Qumran type community. Georg Stecker believed he was a Gentile. O. Lamar Cope more recently argued that he was a Christian Jew familiar with the Hebrew Bible and an expert in the contemporary Judaic interpretation of it.[11]

Although, some New Testament scholars place Matthew outside Judaism,[12] scholars such as Bornkamm and Barth believe that Matthew was written before the break from the Synagogue; thus, Matthew is a Jewish document.[13] In a similar vein, Saldarini contends that the writer is from a Jewish sect found in greater Syria.[14] It may have been composed from multiple sources; however, the redactor was certainly familiar with both Jewish and Jewish-Christian theologies. Richard Bauckham points out, "Most New Testament scholars would now agree that the New Testament writings belong wholly within the Jewish world of their time."[15] The preponderance of research evidence suggests that Matthew's composition correlates with an authorship date of approximately 80 CE. This would support Bauckham,

---

[11] Phillip Sigal, *The Halakhah of Jesus of Nazareth according to the Gospel of Matthew* (Atlanta, GA: Society of Biblical Literature, 2007), 13.

[12] Charles H. Talbert, *Reading the Sermon on the Mount* (Columbia, SC: University of South Carolina Press, 2004), 3.

[13] Ibid.

[14] Anthony J. Saldarini, *Matthew's Christian-Jewish Community* (Chicago: The University of Chicago Press, 1994), 198.

[15] Richard Bauckham, *The Jewish World Around The New Testament* (Grand Rapids, MI: Baker Academic, 2008), 1.

indicating that New Testament works "authored and/or addressed to non-Torah observant Gentile Christians" are still from within the Jewish world of ideas.[16]

1.2 **Structure of Dissertation**

The purpose of this dissertation is to explore, by contextual and cultural examination, the likely original political interpretation of Jesus' Sermon on the Mount with regards to peace sayings. Chapters cover the context of the Sermon and its listeners, the contemporary thought of the day, the Sermon itself, and the implications of the peace sayings as received by its audience.

1.3 **Findings**

This dissertation will argue that, in the Sermon on the Mount, a very Jewish Jesus – a man true to the religio-political views of his day – reaffirms a Jewish ethical form of non-violent resistance. The most important evidence available is the Gospel of Matthew itself, Jewish ethical writings such as *Pirkei Avot,* other *Mishna* writings, and writings on the *lex talionis.* The evidence points to an audience that would have perceived Jesus as teaching non-violence in a context of resistance rather than completely passive submission. That this is the most plausible interpretation is evident from a comparison of the Gospel account with the oral law. The evidence will demonstrate how Jewish political ideologies regarding peace had opposed the Roman Empire since the fall of the Hasmonean Dynasty and had fostered a climate of political discontent. This discontent reflected the resolution of the Jewish people to overcome their oppression. However, some such as Bar Kochba and Judas Maccabee fought for political liberation of the people, while others, as seen in the Dead Sea Scrolls, capitulated and created eschatological stories to cope with an oppressive political regime. The *mitzvoth* of the listeners reflect the ethical and political ideologies of those who listened to the Sermon. Often commentaries depict Jesus as not being politically orientated —neither for nor against

---

[16] Ibid.

either Rome or the Jewish temple leadership. In contrast, this dissertation argues that Jesus utilizes Jewish ethical and intellectual thought to influence the political ideology of those who heard him speak. The overall finding of this dissertation will be that the writer of Matthew depicts a Jesus who, in style, form, and content, builds on a Jewish ethical foundation to promote non-violent assertion of equality and human dignity in the widely known and oft-cited Sermon on the Mount.

CHAPTER 2

JEWISH ETHICAL AND POLITICAL THOUGHT AT JESUS' TIME

2.1 Introduction

This chapter looks at Jewish peace sayings prior to and during the life of Jesus. Its purpose is to outline the context in which the listeners to the Sermon on the Mount would have interpreted the message of the Jewish Jesus. It covers topics thematically rather than chronologically, researching the biblical models of the *moshiach* (the foretold Messiah figure), a peaceful kingdom, ethical judicial systems, and Jewish principles of warfare and peace. The Jewish understanding of peace in a peaceful kingdom and the definition of justice through the application of the Mosaic law, such as the rules and laws found in the Torah in regards to lending and collateral, are diverse, varied, and not unified. This chapter will explore post-biblical Jewish writings such as the apocryphal writings, the *Mishna Avot,* and the Pseudepigrapha. Political thought in the oral law and *Pirkei Avot* (Chapters of the Fathers) will be examined to highlight connections between Jewish *mitzvoth* of love, peace, and justice and the Sermon on the Mount. The *Pirkei Avot* will be explored in detail to understand how Jewish intellectual thought at the time of Jesus created a unique political ideology of peace as a matter of self-preservation. This chapter demonstrates how *Pirkei Avot* as a compilation of the oral law reflects the sacredness of Jewish tradition. This chapter also looks at political thought and peace sayings found in the Dead Sea Scrolls. Other eschatological writings in the Pseudepigrapha are explored through the Jewish definition of *lex talionis* and the application of *tzedakah*, which is 'charity' in Jewish ethical and political thought. The Hebrew Bible (Torah) also contains peace sayings that would have influenced the listeners to the Sermon and these will be examined too.

2.2 **Biblical Sources for Ethical Thought and Peace**

There are numerous sources in the Hebrew Scriptures for ethical thought on peace. The peace sayings found in the Torah develop the Jewish intellectual understanding through just judiciary systems and lending laws. The resulting understanding of the biblical peace sayings connects the concepts of the messiah figure *(moshiach)*, peaceful kingdoms, ethical judicial systems, and the policy of warfare.

2.2.1 Biblical *Moshiach* and a Peaceful Kingdom

To the fore in the minds of the Jewish listeners to the Sermon on the Mount would have been the biblical understanding of *moshiach* and the peaceful kingdom.[17] The Jewish people already had an understanding of what this future king would be like through two different concepts of *moshiach*.[18] The first is a *moshiach* that is eschatological in nature, and the second is Davidic in style.[19] The *moshiach* in Jewish eschatology and in the Dead Sea Scrolls is the future king who comes from the Davidic line and who will rule in the messianic age of peace.[20,21] Texts defining the characteristics of the *moshiach* according to Dead Sea Scroll eschatology have been found in the Cairo *Genizah* and in the Community Rule from Cave 1.[22] The Dead Sea Scrolls are a collection of 972 texts discovered between 1946 and 1956 at *Khirbet* Qumran in modern day Israel. These scrolls provide glimpses of the intellectual thought over different periods of time. The Cairo *Genizah* is from a later date than the

---

[17] Daniel Boyarin, *The Jewish Gospels* (New York: The New Press, 2012), 72.

[18] Ibid.

[19] Robert H Eisenman and Michael Wise, *The Dead Sea Scrolls Uncovered* (New York: Barnes and Noble, 2004), 17.

[20] Ibid.

[21] The Community Rule (1QS), which was previously referred to as the Manual of Discipline and in Hebrew *Serekh ha-Yahad* is one of the first scrolls to be discovered near *Khirbet* (ruin of) Qumran. The Rule of the Community is a key sectarian document and is seen as definitive for classifying other compositions as sectarian or non-sectarian.

[22] Ibid.

Sermon on the Mount but the documents complement the Dead Sea Scrolls.[23] The Scrolls

provide different interpretations of Jewish society, groups, practices, and beliefs at the time

of Jesus and the early Christians.[24] Scholars such as Yizhar Hirshfeld contend that the

Qumran community where the scrolls were found may or may not have been Essenes,

because archaeology at the site shows four different periods of development and

civilization.[25] This point is challenged by Taylor, who contends that the most plausible

conclusion is that they were Essenes.[26] Essene authorship of the scrolls has been the long

standing theory.[27] The text *Miqsat Ma'ase ha-Torah* (lit., "Some Rulings Pertaining to the

Torah"), also known as 4QMMT, changes the view of the Essene hypothesis.[28] 4QMMT,

which was revealed in 1984, contains 22 laws indicating why the group broke away from the

Jerusalem establishment and what it would take for them to go back to Jerusalem.[29] These

laws show that the Essene group (as seen in Talmudic sources) was part of a break-away

Sadducean group who left the Hasmonean high priest control after the Temple revolt of 168 –

---

[23] The Cairo *Genizah* documents include both religious and secular writings composed from about 870 AD to as late as 1880 and found in the *genizah* or storeroom of the *Ben Ezra* Synagogue in Fustat or Old Cairo, Egypt. The normal practice for *genizot* (pl. of *genizah*) was to remove the contents periodically and bury them in a cemetery. Many of these documents were written in the Aramaic language using the Hebrew alphabet.

[24] Amy-Jill Levine, Dale C Allison Jr and John Dominic Crossan, *The Historical Jesus in Context* (Princeton, NJ: Princeton University Press, 2006), 112.

[25] Yizhar Hirschfeld, *Qumran in Context: Reassessing the Archaelogical Evidence* (Peabody, MA: Baker Academic, 2004).

[26] Joan E. Taylor, "Review Article Qumran in Context: Reassessing the Archaeological Evidence," *Bulletin of the Anglo-Israel Archaeological Society* 25, number 1 (2007): 182.

[27] The Essene hypothesis suggests that the scrolls found in Qumran were written by the community which kept and preserved the documents. Taylor's work does show how the caves in Qumran have had multiple groups living in them; however, the Scrolls date to the time during which the Essenes occupied the caves and created settlements in the area. Schiffman also questions the hypothesis saying it is in serious need of reevaluation.

[28] Schiffman, *Qumran and Jerusalem.*

[29] Ibid.

164 BCE.[30] Schiffman suggests that the previous hypothesis needs to be re-vamped to show

that the Essenes were Sadducean sectarians.[31]

The second portrait of a *moshiach* in the Hebrew Bible and in the Dead Sea Scrolls

developed from commentaries (*pesharim*) on Isaiah, Zechariah, Psalms and compendiums of

Messianic proof texts.[32] The expectation of a *moshiach* extends back into the author of

Deutero-Isaiah who tried to identify a Davidic messianic figure in Isaiah 44:23-28 because v.

28 identifies Cyrus as a shepherd.[33] Early Judaism even speculated whether this *moshiach*

was Cyrus the Great (600-530 BCE).[34] Even the great sages such as Hillel during the time of

Jesus sought to identify different people who could be *moshiach*, and subsequently R. Akiba

and Bar Kokhba were questioned as whether they were the Messiah.[35] Further

scholarship within Rabbinic Judaism modified and changed the understanding of a Messiah

to a single person.[36,37]

Christianity developed the interpretation of two messianic lines coexisting in one person

from Numbers 24:17, creating the 'World Ruler' or 'Star' prophecy. Other beliefs

---

[30] Ibid.

[31] Ibid., 32.

[32] Ibid., 18.

[33] Moshe Reiss, "Cyrus as Messiah," *Jewish Bible Quarterly* 40, no. 3 (2012): 159-162.

[34] Ibid., 159.

[35] Matthew V. Novenson, "Why Does R. Akiba Acclaim Bar Kokhba as Messiah," *Journal for the Study of Judaism,* volume number 40, no. 4-5 (2009): 551-572.

[36] Eisenman and Wise, *The Dead Sea Scrolls Uncovered, 18.*

[37] Jewish messianism has its root in the apocalyptic literature of the 2nd century BC to 1st century BC, promising a future "anointed" leader or Messiah to resurrect the Israelite "Kingdom of God", in place of the foreign rulers of the time. This corresponded with the Maccabean Revolt directed against the Seleucids. Following the fall of the Hasmonean kingdom, it was directed against the Roman administration of Iudaea Province, which, according to Josephus, began with the formation of the Zealots during the Census of Quirinius of 6 AD, though full scale open revolt did not occur till the First Jewish–Roman War in 66 AD. Historian H. H. Ben-Sasson has proposed that the "Crisis under Caligula" (37-41) was the "first open break between Rome and the Jews", even though problems were already evident during the Census of Quirinius in 6 and under Sejanus (before 31).

surrounding Numbers 24:17 are seen in the *Deir Alla* inscription which characterizes a two-messiah interpretation since the reference to God is made in Hebrew in the plural form.[38] There, the setting is not monotheistic: we read, for instance, about a gathering of a group of gods. The word *elohim* in the Bible (although a plural word) refers to one God. The same word in the *Deir Alla* text refers to more than one god.

In the diverse world of the Dead Sea Scrolls, a combination of the Aaronic and the Davidic Messiah lines occurs in the Damascus Document, the War Scroll, and the compendiums of Messianic proof texts known as florilegium.[39] It must be noted that in "the Hebrew, Aramaic, and Greek languages, the words for kingdom are all abstract. In the ancient world, kingdom referred to lordship, rule, reign, or sovereignty, not primarily to a geographical area."[40] The Jewish understanding of a kingdom of God includes therefore a *moshiach* who has influence and control over many different peoples, regardless of region.[41] The *moshiach* heralds the promise that David's descendants will rule forever which is interpreted to mean "that the messiah, son of David and son of God (2 Sam 7:14), will himself reign over Israel forever."[42] The tension existing between the Roman state and the Jewish leadership created a political climate ripe for conflict, during the intertestamental period between the last Hebrew Bible prophet Malachi and the New Testament's John the Baptist. A *moshiach* from the Davidic line (Pharisees) was looking to restore the political kingdom of Israel; a *moshiach* from the Levitic line was looking to restore the kingdom

---

[38] The *Deir 'Alla* Inscription (or *Bala'am* Son of *Be'or* Inscription) was discovered in 1967 at *Deir 'Alla*, Jordan. The excavation revealed an inscription on the wall of a story relating visions of the seer of the gods *Bala'am*, son of *Be'or*, who may be the same *Bala'am* mentioned in Numbers 22–24 and in other passages of the Bible. This *Bala'am* differs from the one in Numbers because he is not a prophet of Yahweh but he is associated with Ashtar, a god named *Shgr*.

[39] Ibid.

[40] Scott, *Jewish Backgrounds of the New Testament,* 297.

[41] Ibid., 297.

[42] Bauckham, *The Jewish World Around The New Testament,* 346.

through the line of Melchizedek.[43] Josephus writes in *War* that the world ruler prophecy was the moving force behind the political instability.[44] The *moshiach* influenced the reception of Jesus' peace sayings.[45] It is noteworthy that the *Mishna*, the first major written redaction of Jewish oral traditions dating from c. 220 BCE, contains no definition of the *moshiach*.[46]

2.2.1.1 *A Kingdom of Peace*

An understanding of a kingdom of peace within biblical Judaism is found in Isaiah 9.[47] The prophecy for *moshiach* portrays the type of Davidic descendant required to lead the Jewish kingdom, and the listeners to the Sermon on the Mount would understand that a descendant of the Davidic line was expected as *moshiach*, and these people had a belief system akin to that of the Pharisees.[48] This *moshiach* would lead the people as both head of state and of government. Isaiah 9:5-6 (JPS) states:

> For a child has been born to us,/ A son has been given us./ And authority has settled on his shoulders./ He has been named,/ 'The mighty God is planning grace;/ The Eternal father, a peaceable rule'/ In token of abundant authority/ And of peace without limit/ Upon David's throne and kingdom,/ That it may be firmly established/ In justice and in equity/ Now and evermore./ The zeal of the Lord of Hosts/ shall bring this to pass.

---

[43] Ibid., 311.

[44] Eisenman and Wise, *The Dead Sea Scrolls Uncovered,* 18.

[45] Scott, *Jewish Backgrounds of the New Testament,* 311.

[46] Jacob Neusner, William S. Green and Ernest Grerichs, *Judaisms and their Messiahs* (Cambridge: Cambridge University Press, 1990).

[47] Boyarin, *The Jewish Gospels,* 72.

[48] Scott, *Jewish Backgrounds of the New Testament,* 302.

The kingdom of peace is one whose characteristics would be manifested by a Jewish *moshiach*. This text refers to the Jewish nation state and no other.[49] This prophecy limits a *moshiach* figure to the Jewish nation; it is not appropriate to Gentile (*goyim*) nations.[50]

Other figures in Jewish history identified as a *moshiach* before Jesus included Simon of Peraea, Athronges, and Menahem ben Judah.[51] Similarly, in the period after Jesus, Simon bar Kokhba would be so identified. These *moshiachim* each fulfilled certain elements of Isaiah 9:6-7 and were so identified by people who followed them.

It is very difficult to determine how Jesus' Jewish audience would have interpreted his messianic claims because of the number of messianic figures and because of the disparate sets of Jewish texts that made those claims.[52] The specific texts quoted by the different groups ultimately determined how they understood the messianic figure. Saldarini points out: "Christian interpreters have often attributed to first-century Judaism a univocal belief in an eschatological, political, nationalistic Messiah. In reality, not all Jews believed in an afterlife or an apocalyptic ending to the world. Of those who did, some expected a messianic figure and some did not."[53] This created a great variation in the interpretation of the messiah.

N.T. Wright suggests that the brutal experiences of kings and kingship in Jesus' day inevitably shaped his contemporaries' understanding of the promised messianic figure and pushed it in the direction of a militaristic/conquest figure.[54] Some of the Jewish people, not all, looked for a militaristic *moshiach* to free them from an oppressive Roman empire.

---

[49] Ibid.

[50] Ibid.

[51] See Flavius Josephus, *Jewish Antiquities* 17.278-284, translated by William Whiston, accessed 13 March 2013, http://www.gutenberg.org/files/2848/2848-h/2848-h.htm.

[52] Ibid., 310.

[53] Saldarini, *Matthew's Christian-Jewish Community*, 168.

[54] N. T. Wright, *The New Testament and the People of God* (Minneapolis, MN: Fortress, 1992).

2.2.1.2 *Peaceful People*

Micah 4:1-4 defines the people who are in the kingdom of peace. The Hebrew text is a prophetic message of peace for a future messianic kingdom comprised of people of peace who are in submission to the Jewish Torah and to God.[55] The proclamation that people will no longer learn war but will sit under trees of peace illustrates Micah's expectation of the *moshiach*. Micah 4:1-4 (NRSV) reads:

> In days to come, the mountain of the Lord's house shall be established as the highest of the mountains, and shall be raised up above the hills. Peoples shall stream to it,/ and many nations shall come and say: "Come, let us go up to the mountain of the Lord, to the house of the God of Jacob; that he may teach us his ways and that we may walk in his paths." For out of Zion shall go forth instruction, and the word of the Lord from Jerusalem,/ He shall judge between many peoples, and shall arbitrate between strong nations far away; they shall beat their swords into ploughshares, and their spears into pruning hooks; nation shall not lift up sword against nation, neither shall they learn war any more;/ but they shall all sit under their own vines and under their own fig trees, and no one shall make them afraid; for the mouth of the Lord of hosts has spoken.

The message of Micah 4 brings *shalom* (peace) through a peaceful people heralded through the *moshiach*. The prophetic message of Micah 4 is "profound yet simple: God's shalom brings the promise of a universal peace that is based on justice and the renunciation of bloodshed."[56]

2.2.1.3 *The Jewish Nation and the Kingdom of God*

---

[55] Scott, *Jewish Backgrounds of the New Testament,* 350.

[56] Joseph J. Fahey, *War and the Christian Conscience* (Maryknoll, NY: Orbis, 2008), 32.

Jesus during the Sermon on the Mount discusses the Kingdom of God; however, this concept is not unique to New Testament writings. Judaism historically strived to protect the national identity of the Jewish people. During the lifetime of Jesus, "the Kingdom of heaven, incorporating the restored earthly kingdom of Israel, was seen as the counterpart of the Roman Empire, known as the wicked kingdom."[57] Matthew 6:33 (NRSV) in the Sermon on the Mount states, "…but strive first for the kingdom of God and his righteousness, and all these things will be given to you as well."

Vermes asserts that the concept of the kingdom of God began in biblical Judaism: "The kingdom of God was not invented either by John the Baptist or by Jesus. It grew out of old biblical traditions where it had been developing over centuries."[58] It grew from different concepts: "the ruler of Israel, the Israelite nation as God's people, and the Jewish king as ultimately God's lieutenant ruling over all the nations of the earth."[59]

The kingdom of God developed from the view of the kingship of God over the Jews. Its role was "originally confined to God's dominion over the Jews."[60] Vermes further states that, as the concept of the dominion of God over humankind grew, "the idea progressively expanded to a divine rule over the whole of mankind, since God was the Creator of the whole world."[61] Thus, the understanding by many Jews was that the divine rule of God was over Jews; however, it eventually grew to encompass non-Jews.

The role of the *moshiach* was to establish God's kingship; however, the perception of the person of the king varied with the sect of Judaism defining *moshiach*. The Zealots believed that this kingdom would be established through the use of military might on foreign nations

---

[57] Geza Vermes, *Christian Beginnings From Nazareth to Nicaea, AD 30 – 325* (London: Penguin, 2012), 41.

[58] Ibid., 40.

[59] Ibid.

[60] Ibid.

[61] Ibid.

by the Jewish king.[62] The expanded role of the *moshiach* kingdom was to provide a kingdom on earth, and it was "followed by their [the Jews'] religious subjection of the Deity of the victors, or directly by God without the royal or messianic human agency."[63]

The expansion of the discipleship of the people is through the call for Torah obedience.[64] God's kingdom was established by following the Law of Moses:

> Although the pious and often apolitical rabbis conceived of the establishment of God's realm, it would happen, not through the power of the sword, but through total submission to the Law of Moses. This was to happen—to use their own words—through the acceptance of the yoke of the Torah.[65]

After the Sermon is concluded, Matthew introduces a similar passage in 11:29. The discussion at the time was not *if* one should follow Torah but *which* rabbi was the correct one to follow. Matthew describes Jesus calling for people to follow his ways. The text states (NRSV): "Take my yoke upon you, and learn from me; for I am gentle and humble in heart, and you will find rest for your souls." The expectation of Jesus was that people would follow him.

2.2.1.4 *The Moshiach and the Peaceful Kingdom Obey the Jewish Law*

To appreciate a possible political understanding of the peaceful kingdom, one must look at the *moshiach* and obedience to the Jewish law. Some Jews at the time of Jesus were obedient to the *mitzvoth*,[66] which are defined as good deeds done from religious duty or a precept or commandment. "The community who listened to the Sermon as recorded in the Matthew

---

[62] Ibid., 40-41.

[63] Ibid.

[64] Saldarini, *Matthew's Christian-Jewish Community*, 163.

[65] Geza Vermes, *Christian Beginnings From Nazareth to Nicaea, AD 30*), 41-42.

[66] Saldarini, *Matthew's Christian-Jewish Community*, 165.

tradition would have paid particular attention to Jesus' close relationship with God, his participation in the biblical traditions of Israel, and his fulfillment of God's will in bringing in God's kingdom."[67]

The theological lens through which one reads Matthew determines how the Sermon is applied to the Gentiles. Matthew 28:19-20 (NRSV) reads, "Go therefore and make disciples of all nations, baptizing them in the name of the Father and of the Son and of the Holy Spirit, and teaching them to obey everything that I have commanded you. And remember, I am with you always, to the end of the age." The key to understanding the audience of the Sermon is observance of the law. Saldarini continues, "The Matthean audience of the Sermon on the Mount relates to the nations (gentiles) not through a supercessionist theory developed in the second-century but through law (*mitzvoth*) observance."[68]

The Torah's validity in the eyes of the listeners is important. Matthew 5:17 (NRSV) states: "Do not think that I have come to abolish the law or the prophets; I have come not to abolish but to fulfill." Jesus was not dispelling the law but clarifying discrepancies in the interpretation of the Torah.[69] Jesus was a *mitzvoth* observing Jew, and according to Boyarin: "Jesus kept kosher, which is to say that he saw himself not as abrogating the Torah but as defending it."[70]

2.2.2. Ethical Judicial Systems

The political understanding of Jewish people at the time of Jesus was expressed also through ethical judicial systems. Equality and justice for all Jewish people was imperative for

---

[67] Ibid., 165.

[68] Ibid., 199.

[69] Donald Senior, "Viewing the Jewish Jesus of History through the Lens of Matthew's Gospel," in *Soundings in the Religion of Jesus: Perspectives and Methods in Jewish and Christian Scholarship*, eds. Bruce Chilton, Anthony Le Donne, and Jacob Neusner (Minneapolis, MN: Fortress, 2012), 81-95.

[70] Boyarin, *The Jewish Gospels*, 103.

successful application of Torah. The Torah provided for an ethical judicial system by requiring justice, not just as checks and balances for the Davidic monarchy, but protection for the people. The text of Exodus 22:26 is an example of compassion between two parties who enter into a legal arrangement involving collateral and is relevant to understanding the interpretation by contemporary Jews of the Sermon on the Mount.

2.2.2.1 *Lending, Collateral and Compassion*

The political understanding of moneylending and collateral in the daily practices of the Jews of the time is important for discovering how those listeners understood the Sermon on the Mount in regards to peace. The Torah regulates how Jewish people lent and borrowed money amongst themselves. Moneylending and collateral have two different standards for Jews and Gentiles. In the first standard, the Jewish person was allowed to lend to a non-Jewish person and was allowed to collect a debt from a Gentile. Deuteronomy 15:3 (JPS) states, "You may dun the foreigner; but you must remit whatever is due you from your kinsmen." This law implies that a loan is allowed only to foreigners and prohibited amongst Jews. The use of the word 'foreigner' shows that the Jewish person and the Gentile were under different legal standards.

In the second standard, Jews are prohibited from charging interest when lending to Jewish people. Leviticus 25:37 (JPS) states, "Do not lend him your money for interest, or give him your food for increase." It is forbidden to issue a loan – whether in money or any other item – to a fellow Jew if it involves charging interest. The two prohibitions come together for added emphasis; the one who lends with interest is doubly guilty. In the Leviticus 25:37, there are two Hebrew words for 'interest:' *neshech* and *marbit.* The two ideas are not separate, since *neshech* is the same as *marbit* and *marbit* is the same as *neshech.*[71] Hebrew Scripture uses words with the same meaning and connotation in regards to an increase. This is supported by

---

[71] Meir Tamari, *Al Chet: Sins in the market place* (Brooklyn, New York: The Judaica Press, 1996).

Exodus 22:24 (JPS), known as negative commandment number 237, which states, "Exact no interest from them." This prohibition against charging interest is a way to protect those in need.

There is also a prohibition against borrowing with interest. Deuteronomy 23:20 (JPS) states that "You shall not deduct interest from loans to your countrymen, whether in money or food or anything else that can be deducted as interest." One may not make a loan – whether money or any other item – to a fellow Jew if it involves payment of interest. Had the Torah not specified this prohibition, it would have been possible that the prohibition against lending with interest lies only with the lender, and that the borrower does not transgress (similar to the prohibition against defrauding, where only the defrauder transgresses, not the defrauded). This is in opposition to the view that Jews may lend with interest to Gentiles. The Torah indicates in Deuteronomy 23:21(JPS) that a Jewish person "may deduct interest from loans to foreigners." The 198th *mitzvah* commands a Jew to charge interest from a non-Jew and then to lend him only money, in order that the Jewish lender does not assist him nor give him rest.

Another example is the understanding of Exodus 22:26 as a guideline for loans and collateral. The biblical writings in regards to loan collateral demonstrate the morality of loans for both the lender and the one who borrowed the money. The political thought of the Jewish *Bet Dien*, or "house of judgment," follows Mosaic law. It influenced how people received the Sermon on the Mount because in the Jewish legal system, ethics and morality are legislated through law. Exodus 22:25-26 (JPS) states, "If you take your neighbor's garment in pledge, you must return it to him before the sun sets; it is his only clothing, the sole covering for his skin. In what else shall he sleep? Therefore if he cries out to me I will pay heed, for I am compassionate." This biblical principle regulates the use of attire as collateral for a loan between individuals. If clothing is collateral for a loan and the borrower defaults, a certain level of due process to collect upon the loan is required.[72] One commandment, which is *mitzvah* 241, enhances Exodus 22:26-27. Deuteronomy 24:17 (JPS) states, "Nor shall you take a widow's garment as pawn." Mosaic laws of finance and ethics were upheld during the time of Jesus by the Jewish law courts. It was forbidden for a creditor to take collateral for a debt from a widow—whether she was wealthy or poor.

The collection of the debt sheds light on the political justice due a person in the judicial system. If that person were stripped naked, being naked "would uncover the judiciary injustice."[73] The compassion inherent in the biblical judicial system creates a kingdom of peace as well as a peaceful people by encouraging compassion towards one's own community. The prohibition on lending and retaining collateral is restricted so as to ensure the health and safety of a person, and the Torah also protects the ability of people to cook meals. Deuteronomy 24:6 (JPS) states, "A handmill or an upper millstone shall not be taken in pawn, for that would be taking someone's life in pawn." It is forbidden for a creditor to take food preparation utensils – e.g., grinders, kneading bowls, pots, and knives – as collateral for a debt.

The creditor's nakedness would itself speak volumes about the immoral standards of the lender.[74] An immoral lender is one to avoid in future commerce. As a protection, the Torah also prohibits the forcible taking of collateral. Deuteronomy 24:10 (JPS) states, "When you make a loan of any sort to your countryman, you must not enter his house to seize his pledge." It is forbidden for a creditor to enter the borrower's home and forcibly take collateral for a debt.

---

[72] Roland H. Worth Jr, *The Sermon on the Mount: Its Old Testament Roots* (Mahwah, NJ: Paulist, 1997), 212-213.

[73] Amy-Jill Levine, Dale C. Allison Jr and John Dominic Crossan, *The Historical Jesus in Context* (Princeton, NJ: Princeton University Press, 2006), 12.

[74] Worth, *The Sermon on the Mount: Its Old Testament Roots,* 216-217.

Loans were to be non-interest principal-only advances from the moneylender to the person borrowing money.[75] The text indicates that when a neighbour's garment was used in a pledge, the lender was obliged return it daily before the coolness of dusk. Guidelines and limitations governed the securing of the collateral required by lenders. The biblical mandate to "return a cloak" allowed protection for both the creditor (who would not be shamed by clients stripped 'naked') and the indebted person (who would have some form of warmth and dignity). Berlin and Brettler demonstrate that the Amos 2:8 and Job 22:6 critique creditors, because "the poorest debtors might have nothing left but the cloaks they slept in."[76] Deuteronomy 24:13 states, "As the sun sets, you shall surely return the pledge to him." A creditor is commanded to return a debt collateral to its Jewish owner when he is in need of it during the daytime – e.g., the tools of his trade or an article of clothing. If the collateral is an item needed by night – e.g., linens, blankets or night wear – he must return it at night and only take possession of it again in the morning, or the man's "nakedness exposes among other things, the oppressor's greed and merciless power."[77]

2.2.2.2 *No Jewish Ethic of War*

Within biblical Judaism, there is no established ethic of warfare, as the Jewish texts advocate self preservation, for both the Israelites of the northern kingdom and the Judahites of the southern kingdom.[78] In Deuteronomy 17:16 (JPS), there is a prohibition against a king accumulating excess horses or acquiring the specialised Egyptian warhorses. This keeps the king's cavalry limited. The Talmud in Sanhedrin 21b comments on Deut. 17:16-17, telling us

---

[75] Ibid., 213.

[76] Adele Berlin and Marc Zvi Brettler, "Deuteronomy," in *The Jewish Study Bible*, ed. Bernard M. Levinson, (Oxford: Oxford University Press, 2004), 157.

[77] Warren Carter, *Matthew and Empire*, (Harrisburg, PA: Trinity International, 2001), 142.

[78] Michael Waltzer, "War and Peace in the Jewish Tradition," in *The Ethics of War and Peace* ed. Terry Nardin, (Princeton, NJ: Princeton University Press, 1996), 96.

that a king can have up to 18 wives, as many horses as he needs for his chariots and mounted troops, and any amount of money in his treasury as long as it is needed for national purposes (and not for his personal fortune). In biblical Judaism, the concepts of war were not developed: "there is no Jewish theory of war and peace, and until modern times, there were no theories produced by individual Jews."[79] During the Second Temple period, there is no ethic or Jewish theory of war; furthermore, the word *milkhama* ('war') is a generalized term for battle.[80]

During the entire period of *Mishnaic* development, there were three types of war models critiqued in Judaism. Waltzer explains:

> The *first* category includes all wars commanded by God; the list is very short, drawn from the biblical accounts of the conquest of the land, though it is subject to some modest rabbinic expansion for the sake of the subsequent defense of the land. The *second* category includes all permitted wars, and seems to be a concession to Israel's kings, since the only examples are the expansionist wars of David. These are the wars that disqualified David from the temple building but they are permitted to him as king… The missing *third* category is the banned or forbidden war. It cannot be the case that all wars not required are permitted, for it is fairly clear that there were wars of which the rabbis disapproved.[81]

War was a medium of self-preservation for the Jewish people. Since Judaism in antiquity lacked a clear guidance for peace and warfare, subsequent interpretations of Jewish peace sayings are varied. The *moshiach* heralds either peace or war; thus, the political and spiritual

---

[79] Ibid., 95.

[80] Ibid., 97.

[81] Ibid., 97.

role of a *moshiach* would impact on how the sayings of Jesus were received.[82] The oral law developed explanations and justifications to explain the ethical and political implications for war. Zealots believed in aggressive fighting, while others sought political peace; thus, by the time of Jesus, the ethical behaviour, motivation or even political persuasion of an individual would determine his opinion about the justice or injustice of a fight.

2.3 **Post-biblical Jewish Writings, Political Thought, and Ethics**

To understand Jewish ethical and peace sayings and the relation that oral law has to the Sermon on the Mount, one must examine *Pirkei Avot* and other post-biblical Jewish writings to see what was redacted at the time of Jesus. There is a strong correlation between the oral law and the sayings of Jesus found in the New Testament. This section will explore those writings to see the influence that Jewish ethics had upon Jewish understanding. The peace sayings in *Pirkei Avot* that teach non-confrontation, loving peace, self-restraint, are part of oral law at the time of Jesus. This section also explores how respect and communitarianism and belief in a single God created a community of Jewish believers who thought fundamentally differently from other peoples in the Roman Empire. Finally, this section also explores how various ideas from the time of Jesus are preserved in the Dead Sea Scrolls.

2.3.1 Oral Law: Dating and Redacting

The *Pirkei Avot* is a compilation of the ethical teachings and maxims of the rabbis of the Mishnaic period. It was an integral part of Jewish ethical development during the period extending from 10 CE up until 220 CE. *Pirkei Avot* is relevant to the time frame of the Sermon on the Mount, because Judah HaNasi redacted it in 220 CE from the oral traditions of rabbinic Judaism known from 536 BCE to 70 CE. Consequently, the *Pirkei Avot* contains sayings of different rabbinic sages who lived at various stages of the *Mishnaic* period

---

[82] Scott, *Jewish Backgrounds of the New Testament,* 311.

(roughly10-220 CE). Schiffman explains that the Second Temple and Talmudic periods paved the way for the Torah-centered rabbinic tradition because they so assiduously cultivated the oral law.[83]

Understanding the relationship between those who lived during the redaction of the *Mishna* and those who heard Sermon on the Mount will increase understanding as to what the latter may have understood. The date of the *Mishna* places the different authors in the same time period as the Sermon on the Mount.

2.3.3.1 *Oral Law: Stages of Development*

The redaction of the oral law occurred in different stages which correlate to the dates of different rabbis who developed ethical sayings. Identifying the different stages of the oral law will help contextualize ethical sayings while providing an understanding of Jewish thought. This era is known as the *Tannaim* period and presents five generations of major writers.[84] Each writer provides ethical and political insight into the context of the Sermon on the Mount. They developed the Jewish ethical laws that became codified in the *Mishna* (the entire body of Jewish law that was passed down before 200 C.E.).

The *Mishna Avot*, therefore, explains how the oral law was handed down from Moses through generations until it was documented. These sayings were current during the time of Jesus.[85] The *Mishna* within *Pirkei Avot* explains that the ethical sayings during the Second Temple period are orally transmitted, and it begins with rabbinic teachings.[86] The oral law has tracts that describe the importance of damages in regards to retributive acts. The development

---

[83] Lawrence Schiffman, *Qumran and Jerusalem*, (Grand Rapids, Michigan: Eerdmans, 2010), 1.

[84] Hillel Gamoran, *Talmud For Everyday Living*, (New York: UAHC, 2001), 1.

[85] Schiffman, *Qumran and Jerusalem*, 1.

[86] Amy-Jill Levine, *The Misunderstood Jew*, (New York: HarperOne, 2007), 27.

of the Talmudic tract known as *Seder Nezikin* deals with damages done toward another; however, *Pirkei Avot* is the only Talmudic tractate to deal solely with ethical and moral principles. Such sources of ethical and moral thought shed light on Jewish socio-political understanding during the time of Jesus. These sources in the *Mishna* define the halakhic system, which in the Second Temple period set out how mainstream Jews were to live by Torah.[87]

Schiffman states that as the "various movements sought to define themselves, they, in turn, intensified their differences in interpretation of scripture and in the attendant practices that they followed."[88] The result is that, during the time of Jesus, the sectarian belief of the people who listened to the Sermon on the Mount rested in Jewish law adherence.[89] These different stages of development moulded thought for Jews at the time of Jesus.

2.3.2 Pirkei Avot and Beginnings

The *Pirkei Avot* provides different examples of how Jewish wisdom literature teaches ethical thought. This *Mishna*, although redacted after the time of Jesus, contains many of the oral sayings and beliefs of Judaism current at the time of Jesus. The sayings explored here are only from those people who spoke during the time of Jesus and not afterwards. The elements of *Mishna* explored are those relevant to the peace sayings in Jesus' Sermon.

The *Pirkei Avot* also reveals similarities between the entire oral law and the Sermon on the Mount. The *Mishna Avot* explores areas such as wisdom, peace, evildoers, and the non-confrontational solutions available to the Jewish person during the time of Jesus. As will now be shown, the *Mishna* teaches a respect of people and a love ethic.

---

[87] Schiffman, *Qumran and Jerusalem*, 5.

[88] Ibid.

[89] Schiffman, *Qumran and Jerusalem*, 5.

2.3.2.1 *Seek Wisdom and Counsel*

Jewish wisdom literature teaches that one should diligently seek wisdom and counsel. *Pirkei Avot* 1:4 states: "Yosi ben Yoezer of Zeredah said: Let your house be a meeting house for the sages, and sit in the dust of their feet, and drink in their words with thirst."[90] Yose ben Yoezer may have been a contemporary of Jesus. The custom at the time of Jesus was to sit at the feet of the sages who taught, as Mary of Bethany did (Luke 10:39).[91] During the period of the Hasmonean controversies (approximately 140 to 116 BCE), scholars - beginning with Jose of Zeredah - were exiled to various places by decrees issued by Antiochus Epiphanes.[92] This led to a decrease in the number of sages at the feet of whom one could sit and learn. As the leadership was exiled, Judah Maccabaeus rose to prominence. In 140 BCE the Hasmonean Dynasty began under the leadership of Judah Maccabaeus, who served as ruler, high priest, and commander in chief. Simon, who was assassinated a few years later and formalized what Judas had begun, established a theocracy as the political system. Hanan Eshel indicates that scholars have different opinions about the importance of the nine decades of Hasmonean rule of Judaea (152 – 63 BCE); some consider this period to be unimportant while others see it as the most influential period of Jewish political independence.[93] This institution of a theocracy under the Hasmonean rule separated Jewish lands from Greek and Roman leadership. Maccabaeus purged the country of Hellenism, and the Hasmonean kings became kings of Judah who combined three functions: secular, military and religious leadership. After the Hasmonean Empire fell, rural life remained relatively unchanged. Cities such as Jerusalem rapidly adopted the Greek language, games and sports, and in more subtle ways adopted and absorbed the culture of the Hellenes. Even the high priests bore such

---

[90] Rami Shapiro, *Ethics of the Sages,* (Woodstock, VT: Skylight Paths, 2006), 7.

[91] Ibid., 6.

names as Jason and Menelaus. Internal political and religious discord ran high, however, especially between the Pharisees, who interpreted the written law by adding a wealth of oral law, and the Sadducees, an aristocratic priestly class who called for strict adherence to the written law, and the Essenes who practised ritual purity.

The exiled sages and leaders in the Diaspora provided ethical insight into peace sayings at the beginning of the Common Era. These insights became valuable at the time of Jesus as those who had learned the oral tradition and Pharisaic teachings balanced learning at the feet of the sages. Thus, at the beginning of this period of time, the scene was set by scholars for listeners to cherish and hold wisdom and counsel close. Teachings, both oral and written, were highly valued and greatly revered. Some of the Jewish listeners to the Sermon on the Mount would have understood that there is a mandate in oral law to seek wisdom and counsel.

2.3.2.2 *Distance Yourself from Evildoers*

The rejection of retribution found in the Sermon on the Mount closely relates to the Jewish ethical statements in *Pirkei Avot*. Some of the Jewish listeners to the Sermon on the Mount would have understood that the *Pirkei Avot* teaches that maintaining an ethical and moral life requires not seeking retribution against another person, not even a wicked person. The ethical-political advice of the *Avot* teaches that a person should avoid association and fellowship with the wicked and should also avoid acts of retribution. *Pirkei Avot* 1:7 states: "Nittai the Arbelite said: keep far from an evil neighbor, and do not associate with the wicked; and do not despair about retribution."[94] Some translations have "Nittai of Arbel teaches, distance yourself from a bad neighbor, do not collaborate with evil, and do not despair of justice."[95] Nittai was probably a shortened form of Natanya; Arbel or Arbela is in

---

[94] *Pirkei Avot* 1:7.

[95] Shapiro, *Ethics of the Sages,* 9.

Galilee near Tiberius.[96] Natanya was the vice president of the Sanhedrin over which Joshua (Mishna 6) presided.[97] This Galilean thought that the righteous should shun the negative influence of the unrighteous.

The *Mishna* teaches that one should distance oneself from evildoers. *Pirkei Avot* 1:7 suggests such a lifestyle. Associating with evildoers creates the propensity to adopt views of the evildoer as well as to mimic the wrongs that person commits.[98] The intent of the *Avot* is to keep temptation from people who may be inclined toward wrongdoing by providing guidance for those who may fall into the temptation of acting unjustly toward other people.[99] According to rabbinic understanding, retribution could be served out by humanity during one's lifetime or could be delivered at a time of judgment by God. This view of retribution allows a person who has been wronged to receive justice, even if persons wronged never experience vindication during their lifetime. Judgment and retribution falls hardest upon those who harden their hearts.[100] Hillel's interpretation examines retribution in light of sin: "the sinner experiences a sort of pleasure and enjoyment in his sin and believes that he is immune to retribution."[101] Thus, some of the Second Temple Jewry would very likely have embraced the idea of distancing oneself from the wicked and avoiding human retribution, both themes prominently addressed in the Sermon on the Mount. When we interpret the Sermon on the Mount's discussion of retribution through the understanding found in oral law, we find that personal retribution is regulated under Jewish law and that association with

---

[96] Toperoff, *Avot,* 31.

[97] Ibid., 41.

[98] Kravitz and Olitzky, *Pirke Avot,* 6.

[99] Ibid.

[100] Toperoff, *Avot,* 43.

[101] Morris Mandel and Samson Krupnick, *Torah Dynamics*, (Spring Valley, NY: Feldheim, 1991), 118.

someone who is doing wrong is forbidden; that way, one will not be tempted to commit a wrong.

2.3.2.3 *Pirkei Avot and Loving Peace*

The *Mishna* principle of loving peace found in *Pirkei Avot* is important for understanding Jewish listeners' likely interpretation of the Sermon on the Mount at the beginning of the Common Era. Peace sayings at the time of Jesus were intended for self-preservation under Roman rule. Hillel was the head of the synagogue, known for teaching love and peace as an ethical and righteous standard of living. *Pirkei Avot 1:12* states, "Hillel and Shammai received transmission from Shemayah and Avtalyon. Hillel teaches, 'discipline yourself in the way of Aaron, loving peace and pursuing peace, loving people and bringing them to Torah.'"[102] Hillel taught that loving peace, pursuing peace, and obeying the Torah are imperative for Jewish listeners. Hillel describes discipline as part of loving and pursuing peace. The medium by which one disciplines oneself in the ways of Aaron is unclear; one view is that "to walk the way of Aaron is to take refuge in peace."[103] Some translations substitute the word 'Torah' for the word 'law', while others translate the phrase as "just moral laws."[104]

Torah scholars have expounded upon love and the pursuit of peace in the domestic context. Loving peace begins in the home where *shalom bayit*, domestic bliss, reigns supreme, thus helping to build and strengthen Jewish family life."[105] Appreciation of peace in the wider community begins at home, and loving peace cannot be understood in a wider context until it is mastered in an intimate one.

---

[102] Shapiro, *Ethics of the Sages*, 13.

[103] Ibid., 12.

[104] Philip Blackman, *Tractate Avoth,* (Gateshead, UK: Judaica, 1979), 44.

[105] Toperoff, *Avot,* 53.

The descendant of Hillel, Rabban Shimon ben Gamaliel, who lived from 10 BCE to 70 CE, continues the peace sayings further. *Pirkei Avot* states, "Rabban Shimon ben Gamaliel teaches, three things ensure the world's survival: justice, truth, and peace, as it is said, speak truth, establish peace, and render honest judgments in your gates."[106] Shimon ben Gamaliel was the grandson of the great sage Hillel and father of Rabban Gamaliel. The sayings of Shimon ben Gamaliel would have been first uttered within the lifespan of Jesus and the apostles. Shimon ben Gamaliel was killed by agents of Rome in 50 C.E. These peace sayings were current during the time of Jesus.

2.3.2.4 *Seeking Non-Confrontational Solutions*

Non-confrontation was part of the intellectual foundation for Jewish peace sayings. Non-confrontation involves maintaining safe boundaries between private individuals and those in authority. Confrontational solutions, such those pursued during Bar Kokhba's rebellion from 132 -136 CE ultimately ended in failure and death. *Pirkei Avot* teaches that one should not seek confrontation. The *Mishna Pirkei Avot* states, "Shemaiah and Avtalyon received [Torah] from them. Shemaiah said: 'Love work; hate authority; and do not become too well known to the ruling power.'"[107] Shemaiah was one who kept authority and its figures at a safe distance.[108] Shemaiah, who was *nasi* (prince or captain) at the end of the Hasmonean period and at the beginning of the Herodian (the first century BCE), was a student of Shimon ben Shatach and had very negative experiences with King Tannai,[109] which affected his view of authority. Shemaiah concluded that it was best to steer a course that did not clash with

---

[106] Shapiro, *Ethics of the Sages,* 17.

[107] *Pirkei Avot* 1:10.

[108] Mandel and Krupnick, *Torah Dynamics,* 69.

[109] Ibid.

authority,[110] and taught that people should not come into conflict with authority as they had no power in the political establishment. Those who sought an amalgamation of leadership combining the spiritual and political were at odds with the Roman Empire; however, those who sought only spiritual leadership could cohabit with Rome, while the Essenes sought both. This political interpretation of non-confrontation is important in relation to interpreting the Sermon on the Mount from a Jewish listener's point of view. Thus, an understanding of existing interpretations of non-confrontation could mould how those who listened to the Sermon perceived the words of Jesus.

2.3.2.5 *Self-Restraint*

The oral law provides guidance for self-restraint and temperament that defines ethical behaviour for the observant Jew. The ethical peace sayings in the *Avot* demonstrate how a Jewish person may respond to conflict. *Pirkei Avot* teaches self-restraint and temperament development through ethical sayings which are also present in the Sermon on the Mount. An example of self-restraint comes from Hillel: "a boor cannot fear sin; and an ignorant man cannot be pious, nor can the shy person learn, nor can the impatient person teach. One who engages excessively in business cannot become wise. In a place where there are no men, strive to be a man." (*Pirkei Avot* 2:6). In order to understand *boor* [בּוֹר] the *Mishna* looks at *haaretz* to define boor, which literally translates as 'people of the land'. There are various interpretations of *Pirkei Avot* 2:6, such as, "authorities differ as to the precise meaning of *am haaretz*, but as it follows the boor, it obviously means an ignorant person or one who disregards the *Halakha* [or the ethical walk]."[111] Subsequent Jewish understandings of the word 'boor' include a person who lacks wisdom or ethical qualities.[112] *Pirkei Avot* 2:6

---

[110] Ibid.

[111] Toperoff, *Avot,* 92.

characterises the temperament of a self-restrained person as one who can spend time in Torah study and who practises self-restraint and develops a peaceful temperament. Nothing indicates that those who heard the Sermon were intellectual or studied. Matthew 5:1 only describes those who heard the Sermon on the Mount as *crowds*. But a person who is well studied in Torah follows the Torah; thus, someone who practices self-restraint is practicing Judaism.

A second example of self-restraint and temperament development found in *Pirkei Avot* relates to anger. Anger as a reaction must be qualified. This understanding of anger for the Jewish listener to the Sermon on the Mount emanates from the way the oral law recommends controlling anger which is an emotional response to another person. For the first century Jewish person versed in oral law, anger was a volatile emotion that needed control. *Pirkei Avot 2:15* gives a list of instructions:

> Rabbi Eliezer said: 'let the honor of your fellow be as dear to you as your own. Do not easily become angry. Repent one day before your death [which could be at any time]. Warm yourself before the fire of the sages, but be careful of their glowing coals lest you be burned, for their bite is the bite of a jackal and their sting the sting of a scorpion and their hiss the hiss of a serpent, and all their words are like coals of fire' (*Avot* 2:15).

The principle of anger management in *Pirkei Avot 2:15* is expressed like this: "Do not be quick to anger". Self-restraint enables one to avoid acting in anger: "We must be level headed enough to assess whether the incident actually sparked true cause for outburst. We should actively attempt to find reasons not to be angry."[113] One is not advised to shun anger completely; every quality God has planted within us is good, so anger should be utilised

---

[112] Kravitz and Olitzky, *Pirke Avot,* 21.

[113] Moshe Lieber, *The Pirkei Avos Treasury.* vol. 1, (Brooklyn, NY: Mesorah, 1997), 106.

judiciously and carefully. The Jewish listeners to the Sermon on the Mount could understand that anger toward one's enemy must be controlled and moderated. Being upset with the Roman Empire was understood as human nature.

2.3.2.6 *Ethical Service does not Expect Reward*

Jewish ethics at the time of Jesus teaches that true service does not expect reward. Jewish understanding of serving one's neighbour is selfless giving to others. The Jewish listener to the Sermon on the Mount would have interpreted the sayings of Jesus to understand that obedience to the political state does not bring a reward but should be done because the state is the ruler over the listener to the Sermon. True ethical service does not expect reward because the giving is done for the sake of the person one is giving to. *Pirkei Avot* 1:3 states: "Antigonus of Socho received it [Torah] from Shimon *HaTzadik* (Shimon the Just). He admonished: 'be not like servants who serve the master for the sake of receiving a reward, but be like servants who serve the master not for the sake of receiving a reward; and let the reverence for Heaven be upon you."[114] Some translations say, "let the fear of Heaven be upon you."[115] The term 'fear' translates as "not mean[ing] dread, but that something is full of awe, wonder and the might of God."[116] There is an implied understanding that reverence for God should exist; however, even though reward and punishment gives parameters for obedience, that should not impact on the ethical choices a person makes. *Pirkei Avot* 1:3 indicates that serving God is not reward-based, "calculation of gain and loss should not determine the ethical act; nevertheless, all human acts are played out before God."[117] Even though

---

[114] *Pirkei Avot* 1:3.

[115] Kravitz and Olitzky, *Pirke Avot,* 3.

[116] Toperoff, *Avot,* 9.

[117] Kravitz and Olitzky, *Pirke Avot,* 3.

obedience requires reward and punishment, the acts of obedience must be ethically and morally sound actions which are founded upon the observance of Torah and the *mitzvoth*.

2.3.2.7 *Respecting Others*

Respecting other people and loving one another rest solidly in the oral law. The listeners to the Sermon on the Mount would have understood the respect due to fellow believers. Respect for other persons is required for ethical behaviour in *Midrash*. *Pirkei Avot* teaches that one is to treat another's property as respectfully as one would one's own. *Pirkei Avot* quotes Rabbi Yosi: "Let the property of your fellow be as dear to you as your own. Qualify yourself for the study of Torah, for the knowledge of it is not yours by inheritance. Let all your deeds be done for the sake of Heaven."[118] Honouring personal property and the rights of others was important. Respecting other people includes respecting their property. With Mosaic law dictating that one is to respect the property of one's neighbour, the Jewish listener would balance the Sermon's *turn the other cheek* with personal convictions. The implications of respecting another's property created categories of people who had integrity towards other people; thus, the listeners to the Sermon could understand the fundamental imperative to act with integrity towards one another. Since Jesus is talking possibly to a Jewish and non-Jewish audience, his peace sayings extend to all people who choose to follow him.

2.3.2.8 *Retributive Justice in Pirkei Avot*

The oral law in *Pirkei Avot* expounds on the ethics of 'doing unto others' just as the famous Golden Rule does. *Pirkei Avot* teaches how one should respond to negative actions. *Avot* 2:7 states: "he [Hillel] also saw a skull floating on the surface of the water. He said to it: because you have drowned others, you were drowned, and in the end, those who have

---

[118] *Pirkei Avot* 2:17.

drowned you will themselves be drowned."[119] The *Mishna* states that "Rashi in Suk. 53a explains that the skull had been severed from the body with the victim identified as a robber who was himself murdered by other brigands."[120] Hillel's comment indicates that the floating skull had a personal aspect to it: "Hillel probably knew the identity of the deceased."[121] The *Mishna* teaches the lesson of retributive justice in this story.[122] Hillel's talking to the corpse shows the extent of retribution: "you were killed because you killed others, and those who killed you will themselves be killed."[123] The Golden Rule echoes this aspect of *doing to others* what one wants to be done to oneself. Retributive justice in *Pirkei Avot* provides a component of the Jewish intellectual thought at the time of Jesus through the oral law.

2.3.3.9 *Love Work and Avoid Conflict*

The oral law teaches a work ethic that avoids conflict with the rulers. Fundamental to Jewish ethical teaching is the understanding that people are to love work and avoid conflict. The ethical teachings of work are found in *Mishna* and instruct readers to avoid conflict with rulers.

Shemaiah and Avtalyon were sages who lived before the *Mishna* was written down, who converted to Judaism from the Assyrian religion and who were descendants of King Sancheriv (2 Kings 19:36) of Assyria. Known as the *zuggot* (the 'couples') they developed understandings of the oral law. Shemaiah was the leader of the Pharisees in the first century BCE and president of the Sanhedrin during the reign of Herod the Great and his writings may have influenced the Jewish audience who listened to Jesus. The *Mishna Pirkei Avot* 1:10

---

[119] *Pirkei Avot* 2:7.

[120] Toperoff, *Avot*, 95.

[121] Kravitz and Olitzky, *Pirke Avot*, 22.

[122] Toperoff, *Avot*, 95.

[123] Eliyahu Touger, *Maimonides Pirkei Avot*, (New York: Moznaim, 1994), 83.

discusses work and authority. This same maxim of loving work and avoiding conflict resonates in the Sermon on the Mount (explored in further detail later in this dissertation). The phrase *hate authority* calls for a critical attitude toward authority. This juxtaposes with Jesus' message of *loving your neighbour*, while the *Avot* teaches a non-violent peace saying by expounding on how not to become noticed by the rulers.

2.3.4 Communitarian Mindset

The oral law teaches an understanding of communitarianism, which is integral to Jewish practice and living. Living in community and avoiding isolation are ethical mandates in the *Mishna*. In *Pirkei Avot* 2:5, it states that Hillel said: "do not abandon community."[124] Building a strong community is a fundamental part of Jewish ethics. *Pirkei Avot* records the communitarian mindset common amongst Jews at the time of Jesus. All Jewish men are to study Torah in synagogues. It is incumbent on the person to grow in an ethical community that takes care of the people with whom one lives. A person who does not join the community in the time of danger and trouble "will never enjoy the Divine blessings."[125] When writing the Talmud, Rashi, whose name was Shlomo Yitzhaki, explained: "if there are no other persons available to respond to the needs of the community, then you must do it. If there are indeed others, then devote yourself to study."[126] Rashi's statement indicates that the need for a community ethic outweighs even the need for Torah study. The Jewish listener to the Sermon on the Mount would process the teachings of Jesus through the context of being in a community of like-minded believers, which is evident in multiple scriptural texts. Examples include the disciples living and working together. Also, the Triumphal Entry of Jesus into Jerusalem (Matthew 21:8-11) is an example of likeminded people following a

---

[124] Shapiro, *Ethics of the Sages,* 21.

[125] Toperoff, *Avot,* 89.

[126] Kravitz and Olitzky, *Pirke Avot,* 22.

prophet they supported. Since the people overwhelmingly accepted Jesus as a prophet, the practice of the community was to associate themselves with likeminded people; thus, followers of Jesus practiced *Avot* 2:5 in this action. Those who were in a community within Judaism associated themselves with like-minded leaders, such as Jesus. This may not be the same group as was at the Sermon; however, his disciples would have been members of both groupings.

2.3.4.1 *Submission to an Oppressive Ruler*

The oral law at the time of Jesus teaches that people should submit to rulers. The *Mishna* teaches that people should patient with the ruling government. The writings in *Pirkei Avot* by Rabbi Yishmael advise followers against overreacting to an oppressive political state. Rabbi Yishmael, a master at *Midrash,* was very young during the destruction of the Temple of 70 CE but he learned the oral law from his grandfather, the high priest, Ishmael ben Elisha ha-Kohen, a *tanna* (rabbinic sage) whose sayings were developed during the time of Jesus through the houses of Hillel and Shammai. The *Mishna* advises people on how to act toward an oppressive political regime. In the *Avot*, Rabbi Yishmael says, "Be submissive to the ruler and patient with oppression. Receive everyone with cheerfulness."[127] Rabbi Yishmael lived in the era of Rabbi Akiva during the years 90 CE to approximately 135 CE. Rabbinic Judaism holds that, Rabbi Yishmael was one of the greatest of the third generation of *Tannaim* because he was the first to codify the thirteen hermeneutic principles for Biblical interpretation, and much of the *halachic Midrash (Mechilta* to Exodus*, Sifrei* to Numbers, and part of *Sifri* to Deuteronomy) is a legacy of his academy.[128] This ethical and political ideology encourages Jews to have patience and passively wait for political change because of political oppression from Rome. The need to preserve the cultic rite and the Jewish people

---

[127] *Pirkei Avot* 3:16.

[128] Lieber, *The Pirkei Avot Treasury.* vol. 1, 173.

dominates. This teaching of the sages during the time of Jesus encourages the Jewish listeners to the Sermon on the Mount to be patient with the political situation.

2.3.4.2 *Pray for the Welfare of the Government*

Oral law at the time of Jesus taught that the people should embrace the government through prayer. Fear of the government provided social order and discipline in the people; however, the *Mishna* teaches people to pray for the government in order not to fear it. Prayer for the government empowers the people, allowing an equalization of power between the people and the state because people feel validated by having God hear their prayers. *Pirkei Avot* 3:2 states: "Pray for the welfare of the government, for were it not for fear of it, each person would swallow their neighbour alive." Prayer for the government helps connect the person with the government and the desire for peace in the wider community and in the world. Prayer for peace implies loyalty to the government: "The loyalty of the Jew to every government has been attested to by history."[129] This is typified in the actions of Jesus who taught people to pray for unity as well.

2.4 The Dead Sea Scrolls and Eschatological Political Thought

What do the scrolls found at Qumran, known as the Dead Sea Scrolls, reveal about the Judaism of Jesus' time? They contain a corpus of traditions that changed over time.[130] The Scrolls are best used for understanding Christianity by recognizing that they illuminate various Jewish groups in the Hellenistic and Roman period in Judea.[131] A total of 972 documents were found at Qumran and many different interpretations of scripture are contained in them, with about 20,000 more fragments that have not been pieced together yet. There are many similarities between the Sermon on the Mount and the Dead Sea Scrolls,

---

[129] Toperoff, *Avot,* 138.

[130] Schiffman, *Qumran and Jerusalem*, 5.

[131] Ibid,, 36.

specifically 4Q521.[132] The similarity between the Sermon and the Dead Sea Scrolls centres on sectarianism and apocalypticism.[133]

Christianity inherited apocalypticism from the books of Daniel, Ezekiel, Amos, Zephaniah, and many others during difficult times. This view was echoed by the Pharisees.[134] There are allusions to God's "Spirit hovering over the Meek" and announcing glad tidings to the meek.[135] Eisenman and Wise translate a fragment of 4Q521, 1 Column 2 (1) as, "The Heavens and the earth will obey His Messiah."[136] The Scrolls reveal the variety of Jewish thought within Judaism and the Diaspora. Scholarship has generally identified the Qumran community during the time of Jesus as the Essenes, primarily known from Josephus (*War* 2:567) and Philo (*Prob.*78).

From Josephus, we know of five major sects: Pharisees, Sadducees, Essenes, Zealots and Sicarii. He divides those sects into three groups: philosophical (religious), nationalist, and criminal. Only three are philosophical, while the others are political and religious in nature: "For there are three philosophical sects among the Jews. The followers of the first of which are the Pharisees; of the second, the Sadducees; and the third sect, which pretends to a severer discipline, are called Essenes."[137]

The Essene community maintained the Dead Sea Scroll library; there is no proof that the Essene community authored the documents, but they maintained documents written by vastly different Jewish traditions and groups and moved to Qumran with the intent to preserve and

---

[132] Eisenman and Wise, *The Dead Sea Scrolls Uncovered,* 119.

[133] Schiffman, *Qumran and Jerusalem*, 36-37.

[134] Ibid., 37.

[135] Eisenman and Wise, *The Dead Sea Scrolls Uncovered*, 119.

[136] Ibid., 23.

[137] Flavius Josephus and William Whiston, *The War of the Jews*, 1 chapter 8.2. Lawrence, KS: Digireads.com, 8.

bury scrolls.[138] The Essene community is described by Philo of Alexandria as a group of people who lived in communes, had no private property such as houses, slaves, cattle, ate communally, and shared income in a common fund.[139] Joan Taylor explains that the Essenes were preeminent among Jews in the first century CE and that the community was the choice for men of a certain education.[140] The Scrolls show a dynamic side of Judaism that was mystically-minded and more concerned with spiritual experience, possibly because they may have been a splinter from the Zadokite priests.[141]

The discovery of these scrolls throws some light on Jews who were contemporary to Jesus.[142] The Scrolls indicate how thought was fluid in content and varied.[143] They demonstrate that some groups of Jews, exceeding 4000 people, opposed the Temple system: "The scrolls reflect the creedal concepts of a group of dissenters who propounded an extreme Messianism. They indeed parted company with proto-pharisaic Judaism, but never amalgamated with Christianity."[144] Jassen contends that the Essenes were a sectarian community that "was formed as the result of disagreements over the ritual and cultic maintenance of the temple, which compelled the community to withdraw from the center of Jewish life in Jerusalem."[145] The Essene community opposed corruption of the priestly temple

---

[138] Joan Taylor, *The Essenes, the Scrolls, and the Dead Sea* (Oxford: Oxford University Press, 2012), 195.

[139] Joan Taylor, *The Immerser* (Grand Rapids, Michigan: William B. Eerdmands, 1997), 16-17.

[140] Taylor, *The Essenes, the Scrolls, and the Dead Sea*, 195.

[141] Alison Schofield and James C. Vanderkam, "Were the Hasmoneans Zadokites?" *Journal of Biblical Literature* 124, no. 1 (2005), 73.

[142] Eisenman and Wise, *The Dead Sea Scrolls Uncovered*, 75.

[143] Ibid.

[144] Shemaryahu Talmon, "Waiting for the Messiah: The Spiritual Universe of the Qumran Covenanters," in *Judaisms and their Messiahs*, ed. Jacob Neusner, William S. Green, and Ernest Frerichs, (Cambridge: Cambridge University Press, 1990), 113.

cult in the Jerusalem Temple from the Hasmonean priestly line and a Hellenistic Zadokite priestly line.[146] Disagreements about the purity of the Temple in Jerusalem caused the Essenes to move out of Jerusalem in order to avoid being unclean. The Essene community believed that the Temple was impure and that unless the Temple was purified from impure priests, total destruction of humanity would occur.[147] Jassen clarifies, "There is no evidence that these disagreements ever resulted in violent encounters in Jerusalem. They did, however, eventually solidify the perspective of the community that all 'outsiders' are members of the Sons of Darkness and thus destined for ultimate destruction."[148] Schofield and Vanderkam further state, "We have good reason for believing that the community of the Dead Sea Scrolls, usually thought to be a branch of the Essenes, opposed the Hasmonean high priests. At least one of them they referred to as the *Wicked Priest*, and it is very likely they dubbed Alexander Jannaeus the *Angry Lion*."[149] Other scholars, such as Vermes and Jozef Milik, identify the Wicked Priest as Jonathan the Hasmonean who officiated as high priest in 152-143 BCE.[150] However, Schofield and Vanderkam conclude that "we have considerable reason to believe that the Hasmoneans were a Zadokite family and no evidence to the contrary."[151] Taylor cautions that the Essenes should not be automatically considered to be pacifists or vegetarians.[152] They did though maintain their own legal system according to Mosaic law, and

---

[145] Alex Jassen, "The Dead Sea Scrolls and Violence: Sectarian Formation and Eschatological Imagination," *Biblical Interpretation*, volume 17, nos. 1-2 (2009), 13.

[146] Bruce McComiskey, "Laws, Works, and the End of Days: Rhetorics of Identification, Distinction, and Persuasion in Dead Sea Scroll 4QMMT," *Rhetoric Review* 29, no. 3 (2010), 225.

[147] Ibid., 223.

[148] Jassen, "The Dead Sea Scrolls and Violence," 12.

[149] Schofield and Vanderkam, "Were the Hasmoneans Zadokites?", 80.

[150] Eshel Hanan, *The Dead Sea Scrolls and the Hasmonean State* (Grand Rapids: Eerdmans, 2008), 42.

[151] Ibid., 87.

[152] Taylor, *The Essenes, the Scrolls, and the Dead Sea*, 341.

some honoured the Temple by sending votive gifts but would not have any association with those outside the community.[153]

The Qumran community discouraged violence in the community by focusing on eschatology. Jassen contends that, for the "Qumran community, violence outside of the framework of the eschatological battle is not legitimised and presumably did not exist."[154] The writings of the Qumran community advocated delaying all punishment until the *eschaton*. By developing its eschatological thought, the community defused its own violent actions.[155] The political climate was that of an occupied country and the religious climate was sectarian.[156]

There are many similarities between the character of Jesus and that of members of the Essene community.[157] Taylor suggests that there is no evidence that Jesus or John the Baptist were Essene, nor that they lived at Qumran solely because they shared similar eating habits, dress habits, and location of residence.[158] The similarities are more widespread than that and do not limit Jesus and John the Baptist to an Essene community. The Essenes heralded *moshiachim* to come. These *moshiachim* would fit the eschatology of the Essenes, which is similar to that of some of the listeners: "[The *moshiachim* are] at the forefront of the community's vision of the end of days, which would witness the destruction of the Romans and wayward Jews in an eschatological war."[159] This in no way indicates that Jesus was an

---

[153] Ibid., 198-99.

[154] Jassen, "The Dead Sea Scrolls and Violence," 9.

[155] Ibid.

[156] Ibid.

[157] Ron Pazola, "Can the Dead Sea Scrolls Teach Us About the Living Jesus?" *U.S. Catholic*, volume 58, issue 11, 17 November (1993), 14.

[158] Taylor, *The Immerser*, 48

[159] Jassen, "The Dead Sea Scrolls and Violence," 13.

Essene; it just suggests how those who were Essene may have understood some of the sayings of Jesus in the Sermon and how some of the Sermon's content was similar to documents in the Essenes' scroll library.

Other writings not found in Qumran offer similar apocalyptic views. In 1 and 2 Enoch, the image of an apocalyptic exchange develops between the *moshiach* and the evil powers.[160] Such Jewish apocryphal literature is similar to some Christian literature of the New Testament, especially the book of Revelation.[161] The book of Jubilees, found among the Dead Sea Scrolls, does not have the same view of *moshiach*. Talmon argues that this is juxtaposed to "other Jewish writings written before the Common Era [which] provide evidence of a prophecy of a *Moshiach*, or Messiah figure, who is to establish a kingdom of peace."[162]

The Scrolls themselves contain both types of *moshiach* figures. The first figure is a messiah of Aaron's lineage who is a spiritual leader, and the second is a messiah of Israel (Davidic line) who is a political leader.[163] The Jews who were anticipating a spiritual *moshiach* from Aaron's lineage expected peace among all people.[164,165]

The Sermon on the Mount addresses elements that are brought by a *Messiah*, such as a kingdom of God through peace. However, even those who first heard the Sermon on the

---

[160] George W. E. Nickelsburg, "First and Second Enoch: A Cry against Oppression and the Promise of Deliverance," in *The Historical Jesus in Context*, eds. Amy-Jill Levine, Dale C Allison Jr, and John Dominic Crossan, (Princeton, NJ: Princeton University Press, 2006), 89.

[161] Ibid.

[162] Talmon, "Waiting for the Messiah," 111.

[163] Geza Vermes, *The Real Jesus,* (London: SCM, 2009), 129.

[164] Talmon, "Waiting for the Messiah," 111.

[165] The vision of an anointed king in Hebrew is *masiah* and Greek as *Christos*. There was an expectation that there will be a political and socio-religious faith.

Mount may have taken very different views of the peace sayings because of their differing views of the role of a Messiah.[166]

The Dead Sea Scrolls refer to a kingdom of peace in 4Q246. The scroll written in Aramaic known as 4Q *Aramaic Apocalypse,* also referred to as 4Q *Son of God Text* or 4Q *Pseudo-Daniel* (4Q246), is of particular interest in establishing how Jewish thought saw a kingdom of peace. Only a single fragment containing the remains of two columns of the document, copied in the first century BCE, has survived.[167] This small fragment provides an understanding of messianism. Andrew Lawler suggests that the scrolls provide a sample of the intellectual thought and context in which the listeners to the Sermon understood the Sermon:

> For Christians as well, the scrolls are a source of profound insight. Jesus is not mentioned in the texts, but as Florida International University scholar Erik Larson has noted, the scrolls have "helped us understand better in what ways Jesus' messages represented ideas that were current in the Judaism of his time and in what ways [they were] distinctive."[168]

The Scrolls illuminate Christian thought as followers of Jesus developed elements of Jewish thought. The scrolls show the rich diversity of ways in which the listeners to the Sermon may have understood Jesus by highlighting the variety and diversity of Jewish thought in that era.

2.4.1 Pseudepigrapha and Political Thought of the Peaceful Kingdom

Jewish pseudepigrapha are writings typically ascribed to various Jewish patriarchs and prophets, which were composed within approximately the first two hundred years of the Christian Era. David DeSilva suggests that the Jesus' Sermon was influenced by the book of

---

[166] Talmon, "Waiting for the Messiah," 195.

[167] T. C. Vriezen and A. S. van der Woude, *Ancient Israelite and Early Jewish Literature,* (Leiden: Brill, 2005), 689.

[168] Andrew Lawler, "Who wrote the Dead Sea Scrolls?" *Smithsonian* 40, no. 10 (2010): 40-47.

Ben Sira or the book of Tobit.[169] DeSilva contends that the teachings of Jesus in the Sermon and Tobit demonstrate a similarity between Jewish literature and Jesus' peace sayings.[170] DeSilva further contends that the most significant resemblance between Tobit and Jesus' Sermon concerns obedience to the Torah.[171] This biblical Jewish writing impacts on the thought of Jews who lived during the time of Jesus because the pseudepigrapha, particularly from the Maccabean time, influenced Jewish understanding of Torah observance (which protected the Jewish identity, as seen in Chapter Two).[172]

The pseudepigraphal book of Jubilees describes a political understanding of a peaceful kingdom by Jewish believers at the time of Jesus. It illustrates the divergent context of Jews regarding peace. There is very good reason to accept the accuracy of the book of Jubilees, even though many different pseudepigrapha were created fictionally and not based on true accounts of prior biblical writings.[173] It is "possible that the work was written shortly before the Maccabean revolt of 167–164 B.C.E. It is nevertheless to be dated no later than 140 B.C.E."[174] There is a kingdom of peace that will come for those who observe the Torah:

> Reference to the death of the patriarch provided the author with the opportunity to offer a minor apocalypse in chapter 23 in which the history of the people of Israel from Abraham to the Maccabean period is treated, a period that, according to the author, is to be followed by the eschatological kingdom of peace in which evil shall no longer be found.[175]

---

[169] David A. DeSilva, *The Jewish Teachers of Jesus, James, and Jude* (Oxford: Oxford University Press, 2012), 12.

[170] Ibid., 12.

[171] DeSilva, *The Jewish Teachers of Jesus, James, and Jude*, 70.

[172] Ibid., 71.

[173] Schiffman, *Qumran and Jerusalem*, 392.

[174] Ibid.

The political implication of a kingdom of peace in Jubilees does not encompass messianic ideals. Those who wrote this literature did not support a messianic figure and or afterlife: "There is an element of living by Torah and through obedience, and the kingdom of peace will come. The priestly author of the book of Jubilees clearly did not cherish messianic expectations and made no reference to the resurrection of the dead, but spoke rather of the preservation of the souls of the faithful [1:24; 23:31]."[176] Therefore, it is possible that readers of the book of Jubilees would have expected a kingdom of peace through its peace sayings, while not necessarily looking for the messianic figure as mentioned above. Some Jewish listeners to the Sermon on the Mount may therefore have understood the implications of a peaceful kingdom as coming through their actions and faithful living and not unilaterally through the actions of the *moshiach.*

2.5 *Lex Talionis as Part of Ethical Thought*

Lex talionis is the principle that a person who has injured another is to be penalized to a similar degree – it is commonly express as 'eye for an eye.' Knowledge of the *lex talionis* has contributed to an ancient understanding of the Sermon on the Mount in texts such as Matthew 5:38-42. This section looks at the application of Hebrew texts to human conflict by defining the *lex talionis* and by describing the influence this ancient legal code has had on Jewish ethics. Both the Code of Hammurabi and the *lex talionis* from Roman law in the Twelve Tables define retaliatory justice.[177] These legal precepts from Roman, Mesopotamian, and Jewish law influence how a contemporary listener would see the issue of one slapping or retaliating towards another in Matthew 5:38-42.

---

[175] T. C. Vriezen and A. S. van der Woude, *Ancient Israelite and Early Jewish Literature,* (Leiden: Brill, 2005), 579.

[176] Ibid., 581.

[177] James F. Davis, *Lex Talionis in Early Judaism and the Exhortation of Jesus in Matthew 5:38-42* (New York: T&T Clark International, 2005), 97.

2.5.1 Defining the *Lex Talionis*

The *lex talionis* is literally defined as the law of retaliation; it is a principle of *like-for-like* that appears both in Jewish and Roman law as well as in many Mesopotamian legal codes.[178] It is a biblical principle of retribution found in the Hebrew Scriptures that seeks to create equitable recompense for acts of aggression. The biblical principle, found in Exodus 21:23-5 (JPS), has shaped and moulded theories of non-violence for two thousand years. The text states, "But if other damage ensues, the penalty shall be life for life, eye for eye, tooth for tooth, hand for hand, foot for foot, burn for burn, wound for wound, bruise for bruise." This text is a code by which Jewish "law strives to make punishment for death or injury fit the crime perfectly."[179] "In the world that Israel lived, vengeance was the rule of the day … they were being told that they could exact nothing more than justice."[180] The *talion* (retaliation) restricts the degree of the punishment, though Fahey states that "the concept of 'retaliation' or 'revenge' is often associated with the Law of Talion, giving it a far more negative meaning than was originally intended."[181] Cohn notes that this standard of justice does not give "him license to do wrong" because it restricts the amount of violence which occurs.[182] It balances power and protects the weak from being overrun by more powerful people. The Jewish listener to the Sermon on the Mount would understand the principle of *lex talionis* and process Matthew 5:38 in light of it.

2.5.2 Influence of Roman Law over Jewish Law

---

[178] Ibid.

[179] Berlin and Brettler, *Deuteronomy*, 154.

[180] Worth, *The Sermon on the Mount*, 231.

[181] Joseph J. Fahey, *War and the Christian Conscience* (Maryknoll, NY: Orbis, 2005), 74.

[182] Beryl D. Cohen, *Jacob's Well: Some Jewish Sources and Parallels to the Sermon on the Mount* (New York: Bookman Associates, 1956), 58.

Roman law superseded Jewish law in the courts, except for religious matters, from 63 BCE.[183] In the days of Jesus, Judaea, Samaria, and Idumea did not have independence but had a Roman procurator with full authority over them.[184] The Sanhedrin ruled over local affairs that the Roman procurator did not adjudicate.[185] Listeners to the Sermon on the Mount were under Roman rule and subject to Roman law.[186] Rome codified laws for the land in many forms and one important early document was *The Twelve Tables* from 450 BCE. Its form and function in Roman courts remained valid even in the time of Jesus.

In the Roman courts, the Twelve Tables contain methods of equitable remedies for committing a tort, which is violation of a right. "Roman law of the *Lex Talionis* in the *Twelve Tables* was also a likely factor in the first century… the law allowed the option of either a literal *talion* or a monetary compensation in maiming cases."[187] Under Roman law, the type of punishment and crimes were stipulated. When a violent act (mainly violation of laws) was committed under Roman law, the ruling law of Rome articulated the punishment for the person. Roman law developed severe penalties for physical assault: "*The Twelve Tables* laid down somewhat primitive penalties for various types of physical assault. For a maimed limb, retaliation was allowed if the parties could not settle. For less serious assault, a tariff system operated."[188] In courts for Jewish people after 63 BCE, the penalty for committing a crime of physical assault was monetary compensation under the Mosaic *Bet Dein* system of law. These Jewish law courts utilized a monetary compensation system for retribution instead of

---

[183] Morton Scott Enslin, *Christian Beginnings Part I.* (New York: Harper & Row, 1956), 129.

[184] Ibid.

[185] Ibid.

[186] Hans Dieter Betz, *Essays on the Sermon on the Mount* (Philadelphia, PA: Fortress, 1985), 93.

[187] James F. Davis, *Lex Talionis in Early Judaism and the Exhortation of Jesus in Matthew 5:38-42* (New York: T&T Clark International, 2005), 97.

[188] Andrew Borkowski, *Roman Law* (London: Blackstone, 1994), 323.

physical retribution. Although Roman law and Jewish law both had fiscal methods of compensation, the punishment for violating Torah was a fiscal punishment Roman courts did not provide punishment for violation of Jewish law.

Davis asserts that Roman law focuses on quantifiable retaliation, specifically on the measurable amount of justice that a victim can extract from a person.[189] Judaism's interpretation of retribution shifted to an application of fiscal punishment through fines in lieu of physical punishment.[190] Rome had jurisdiction over all legal matters, and the Jewish courts heard only cases of law that violated Jewish law and were not contradictory to Roman law. Thus, the listeners to the Sermon would understand that Jewish law had applied monetary standards to replace *lex talionis*.

2.5.3 The Code of Hammurabi's Influence on Jewish Law

There is merit in considering one of the earlier sets of laws in the region, the Code of Hammurabi. This is the earliest known written legal code, and was composed about 1780 BCE by Hammurabi, the ruler of Babylon. It was discovered in 1901, carved on an eight-foot high monolith. The harsh system of punishment expressed in this text predates the concept of 'an eye for an eye' found in biblical Judaism. The Code lays out the basis of both criminal and civil law, and defines procedures for commerce and trade. This text was redacted for 1,500 years and is considered the predecessor of Jewish and Islamic legal systems alike. The Code of Hammurabi was well-known in ancient times, influencing much of the culture of surrounding areas throughout generations, and ultimately affecting many of the surrounding regions of the Middle East. Judaism grew in exile in Babylon under different empires; thus, the Babylon Talmud adapted to foreign influence, and the application of the *lex talionis* was

---

[189] James F. Davis, *Lex Talionis in Early Judaism*, 97.

[190] Ibid.

influenced by being in exile. Hence, it is likely that popular contemporary views of the *lex talionis* were influenced indirectly by the Code of Hammurabi, and that it also influenced the audience of the Sermon on the Mount indirectly.

The Code of Hammurabi has parallels to the concept of retribution found in Exodus 21:23-25. The text of Exodus 21 parallels the Code of Hammurabi §230, which states: "If [building structures] kill a son of the owner of the house, one shall put to death the son of the builder.[191] This is a literal use of the *lex talionis*, a standard by which the death of one son is equated to the death of another. The Code of Hammurabi §196 states that "if a man destroy the eye of another man, one shall destroy his eye."[192] The theme of the *lex talionis* is known commonly and referenced consistently across the Semitic tribes. In Exodus 21, the punishment set out is not an "obligatory requirement but a limitation on vengeance."[193] The laws of Mesopotamia contain significant similarities to the *lex talionis,* such as the Babylonian law (Laws of Eshnunan [paragraph 53-55] and, the Code of Hammurabi [paragraph 250-252], but the application of them varies according to the political institution.[194]

2.5.3.1 *Proportional and Retaliatory Justice in the Lex Talionis*

In order to understand proportional and retaliatory justice in the *lex talionis* in Judaism, the application of proportional punishment and retaliatory standards need to be defined. In the Sermon on the Mount, "the formula itself is stated without the first Old Testament element 'life for life' as it had already been separated from the entire formula in the Jewish exegesis and debate. The next two elements in line, 'eye' and 'tooth', are then given

---

[191] Ibid., 93.

[192] W. W. Davis, *The Codes of Hammurabi and Moses* (New York: Cosimo Classics, 2010), 98.

[193] Berlin and Brettler, "Deuteronomy," 154.

[194] Ibid.

prominence in the equation. They represent an ethic of proportional and retaliatory justice."[195] The listener to the Sermon would understand that justice is integral; he would understand Jesus' Sermon as a discourse on justice. The Sermon takes liberties to expand the original standard found in the Torah. Contemporary understanding of the term *lex talionis* has shifted to a standard quite different from the original intent: *lex talionis* has been misunderstood as a standard for retaliatory revenge.[196] The listener to the Sermon on the Mount would understand how just and ethical actions define the character of the person. There is no intent behind the retaliation given, only a sense of justice for the loss by a tortfeasor, the one who has committed a personal injury.

2.5.3.2 *Self-Defence and Retaliatory Action*

Self-defence and retaliatory action can use deadly force only under certain circumstances. The comparison must be drawn between non-violent self-defence by an individual and violence used in self-defence. People maintaining a peaceful lifestyle retained the right to use deadly force in self-defence, according to the *halakah*.[197] The use of deadly force in self-defence is authorised by the *Mishna* as a pre-emptive strike under certain circumstances to protect the self. *Berakot* 58a, 62b states: "if a man comes to kill you, rise early in the morning and kill him first." Rabbinic Judaism was endeavouring to ensure that a person was not unnecessarily victimised by another person who acted in direct violation of the first person's rights. Basically, the theory was that it is better to protect one's own rights, even at the expense of the rights of others, if their actions encroach upon one's own rights or safety, especially when a person is coming to kill you. This is not an unlimited right to kill others.

---

[195] Davis, *Lex Talionis in Early Judaism*, 140.

[196] Ibid., 168.

[197] *Berakot* 58a, 62b.

The premise in *Berakot* and *Tannit 25b* is that forbearance and personal restraint are vital.[198] In Rabbinic Judaism, a person's actions and *mitzvoth* defined the type of person they were, and a person who was forbearing would not arbitrarily kill others around them. At the time of Jesus, the listeners to the Sermon on the Mount would maintain forbearance and personal restraint in their life, as exemplified in Matthew 5:39. Jesus defines how a forbearing person reacts to conflict. Similarly, Jesus' discourse on love defines the character of a person (Matthew 5:43). In different stories in the New Testament, such as that of Zaccheus, there are those who look at their lifestyles and compare them to the sayings of Jesus. In rabbinical commentary, retribution will come to all people, not necessarily immediately: "Ignore the possibility – that retribution will suddenly befall the evil one, for eventually his time will come."[199] This comment originates from the oral law. The person who practised forbearance would weigh the use of retaliation toward another person carefully.

Forbearance from non-peaceful acts and practices would help people develop a greater sense of justice in their lives, as justice (which includes loving God and one's neighbour) was the ultimate virtue. Justice in the context of *Avot* 1:7 is slow; it states: "Do not conspire to prevent the truth or exploit another, and in time justice will prevail, for evil cannot succeed alone. Do not despair because justice is slow; do justice yourself and work for justice in your community, and in the end evil will fall before it."[200]

2.5.3.3 *Palestinian and Babylonian Talmud on the Lex Talionis*

The oral law that was redacted into rabbinic texts after the time of Jesus utilises the two different schools of thought found in the Palestinian and Babylonian *Talmudim*. There are five counts of injury for a tortious act committed by a tortfeasor in rabbinic law; these counts

---

[198] Davis, *Lex Talionis in Early Judaism*, 111.

[199] Lieber, *The Pirkei Avos Treasury*, vol. 1, 29.

[200] Shapiro, *Ethics of the Sages*, 8.

shift the punishment from equal retribution to monetary reimbursement for some wrongs committed in the codified system. The method of using monetary compensation to rectify an injustice for tortious crimes existed in the time of Jesus. The listeners to the Sermon on the Mount would have understood that there were changes to oral law through the influence of Roman law; for example, Roman law limited the enforcement of the Jewish rules to religious matters only. Lachs indicates that an injury has five counts of liability:

> The rabbinic interpretation of the biblical law is, 'if a man wound his fellow man, he thereby becomes liable on five counts: for injury, for pain, for healing, for loss of time, and for indignity afflicted. During this entire period it remained a private wrong, and it was up to the injured party whether or not he would press his claim and demand judgment in the form of a money payment.[201]

Rabbinic interpretation allows for injuries to be enforced in the private realm in lieu of a state criminal punishment; consequently, the law of retribution moves to qualify all damages in the form of monetary damages. However, rabbinic Judaism was split between the literal *talion* (retaliation) and fiscal punishment.[202] Davis concludes, "The strongest evidence that a literal interpretation of the *Lex Talionis* was a viable viewpoint in Judaism comes from R. Eliezer [*b. B. Qam. 83b-84a; Mek. Nexikim Exod. 21*] and Philo [*Spec. Leg. 3.181-183*]."[203] This was argued only in rabbinic Judaism and not enforced; thus, the "option for financial settlement" became the application of *lex talionis*.[204]

---

[201] Samuel Tobias Lachs, *A Rabbinic Commentary on the New Testament* (Hoboken, NJ: KTAV, 1987), 104.

[202] David Instone-Brewer, *Traditions of the Rabbis from the Era of the New Testament Volume 2a* (Grand Rapids, MI: Eerdmans, 2011), 34.

[203] Davis, *Lex Talionis in Early Judaism*, 98.

[204] Ibid.

The Palestinian and Babylonian *Talmudim* each contain texts regarding the *lex talionis*. In the Palestinian *Talmud*, the *y. Baba Qamma* 8.1 discusses the application of fiscal compensation as a replacement for the "eye for an eye" standard. Likewise, in the Babylonian *Talmud*, *b. Ketubot* 32a-33b concurs on the use of a financial penalty. Davis speculates that these texts encourage the use of personal restraint; thus, there is an understanding of non-retaliation.[205] Non-retaliation was a concept of peace within the Judaism at the time of Jesus and the listeners to the Sermon of the Mount may have been privy to this *midrash*.

2.6 *Tzedakah* and Charity

The ethical act of giving charity was entrenched in the Jewish person's way of life and redacted into *Mishna* from the traditions existing to the time of Jesus. The foundations of charity and community giving are in the Torah.

Deuteronomy 15:7 (JPS) is a commandment that stipulates that Jews must be charitable toward the Jewish poor. It states, "If, however, there is a needy person among you, one of your kinsmen in any of your settlements in the land that the Lord your God is giving you, do not harden your heart and shut your hand against your needy kinsman." This commandment is coupled with a second commandment in the Torah that regulates how charitable Jews should be towards others around them. The following verse states, "Rather, you must open your hand and lend him sufficient for whatever he needs." This charity encourages ethical living among all people, a social net for the poor, human dignity, and protection for the poor from the rich. The charity of an individual is important in defining their ethical capacity because it demonstrates the capacity for *loving your neighbour*.

2.6.1. Defining Charity and *Tzedakah*

---

[205] Ibid.

The Hebrew word *tzedakah* translates as 'blameless behaviour, honesty, righteousness, justice, or godliness'. The intent is to care for one's community: "*tzedakah* historically has been instituted to care for those whom one lives around."[206] The word defines how a person should act: "the word for charity in Hebrew is *tzedakah*, from the root word *zedek* meaning 'justice' or 'righteousness.' This definition as understood in the Hebrew connotation implies that the act of giving is 'justice' and 'righteousness' which are desired obligations in obeying [God]."[207] The intent of the word changes when translated into Greek and Latin. Early Greek Bible translations render *tzedakah* as *agape*, the Greek word for an altruistically loving relationship, which was later translated into Latin as *caritas*, the root of our English word 'charity'.[208] The LXX more often translates the word *tzedakah* with *dikaiosune* which means 'righteousness', the condition acceptable to God. *Tzedakah* in the Vulgate translates as *iustitia*, which is 'justice, fairness, equity'.

The word *tzedakah* during the time of Jesus did not carry the meaning implied by the Latin Bible. "When it is translated to the Latin, which developed after the time of Jesus and the Latin *Vulgate* Bible... the word charity [becomes] the Latin word *caritas*, meaning *love*."[209] *Caritas* suggests "a donation made out of affection."[210]

However, the intent in the Hebrew word *tzedakah* is giving to anyone regardless of the emotional feeling towards the beneficiary. Those who have nothing forfeit human dignity when they beg. By the first century of the Common Era, the application of *tzedakah* was through helping the poor, compelled by ethical duty as opposed to sentiment or affection.

---

[206] Jill Jacobs, *There Shall Be No Needy* (Woodstock, VT: Jewish Lights, 2009), 13.

[207] Steven Silbiger, *The Jewish Phenomenon* (Lanham, NY: M. Evans, 2009), 37.

[208] Jacobs, *There Shall Be No Needy*, 43.

[209] Silbiger, *The Jewish Phenomenon*, 38.

[210] Joseph Telushkin, *A Code of Jewish Ethics* (New York: Bell Tower, 2009), 156.

2.6.1.1 *Supporting the Poor Reveals a Person's Ethics in Action*

While the Bible itself does not use the word *tzedakah* to refer to mandated monetary gifts to the poor, the early rabbis—beginning in the first centuries of the Common Era—assumed that *tzedakah* refers to such financial assistance. Given that the rabbis did not find it necessary to justify this definition of *tzedakah,* we may assume that the association of the term with charitable giving was already well established by the beginning of the Common Era.[211]

Tzedakah was given to create a social security net to which all should contribute so that one day, circumstance providing, all might also have a claim. This view of charitable giving is built into Jewish ethical living standards established in *Mishna*. The Jewish believer would donate to charity because they were taught that the act of giving is social justice, which is part of loving humankind. One did not give out of pity for a fellow human, which could dehumanize the receiver. The way one approached charity, by social justice, and not love or pity, would distinguish Jewish ethical behaviour from that of others.

2.6.2 Charity in Community Defines Jewish Ethics

The Jewish believer hearing the Sermon on the Mount would have understood the vital importance of being part of a community. The role that charity plays in one's interactions within the community is vital in *Pirkei Avot* to define one's ethics. *Pirkei Avot* 2:5 states: "Hillel said: 'Do not separate yourself from the community; and do not trust in yourself until the day of your death. Do not judge your fellow until you are in his place.'" The converse is isolating oneself from the community; thus, by *not* separating oneself from the community, a person will not abandon the Jewish way of life.[212] According to *Pirkei Avot*, the oral law at

---

[211] Jacobs, *There Shall Be No Needy,* 43.

[212] Philip Blackmand, *Ethics of the Fathers,* (Gateshead, UK: Judaica, 1979), 48.

the time of Jesus, the role a person holds in life should be community-centered.[213] The welfare of the community was supremely important for the Jewish listener to the Sermon on the Mount. He would have understood that winning the support of the community around him was vital: "working for the welfare of the community aligns the community behind you, strengthening your efforts and maximizing results. And while your success will depend on the support of the community, the credit will be yours nonetheless."[214] The community focus of Jesus is evident as he commonly lived, worked, and travelled in communities instead of remaining in the wilderness. The act of charity to the community around one is not a deed that is self-serving in nature or that generates personal wealth; on the contrary, it sends a signal about taking personal interest in the society around about and the welfare of those therein.

2.6.3 *Tzedakah* Creates a Social Net for the Underprivileged

As mentioned, the role of *tzedakah* is to create fiscal security for those less privileged in the community.[215] The development of *tzedakah* provides those in poverty with items such as grain, fruit, grapes, and crops; the basic needs of society for those who do not have enough to survive are provided by the *tzedakah* of the rich or more capable. The intent of *tzedakah* is a redistribution of wealth to those who do not have food (not to be confused with the 'first fruits' that went to the Temple as tithes and offerings). The *Bikkurim* ("first fruits") is the obligation to offer God one's first fruits on the holiday of Shavuot. The Seder *Zeraim* concerns the obligation to dedicate a certain percentage of one's produce to sustaining the *kohanim* (priests), the Levites (who served in the First Temple), and the poor (who did not

---

[213] Eliyahu Touger, *Pirkei* Avot, (Brooklyn, New York: Moznaim, 1994), 80.

[214] Shapiro, *Ethics of the Sages*, 20.

[215] Worth, *The Sermon on the Mount*, 215.

have land of their own). These are separate actions of charity, but *tzedakah* is not the prime choice harvest that goes to the Temple; however, by devoting ten percent of the increase of one's wealth, they still provided a means of support for the poor, underprivileged or stricken. Other years ten percent of the increase went to the Temple. When juxtaposed with Deuteronomy 15, the mandate is better understood that *tzedakah* must be given as charity, in accordance with social justice, at least once every three years, which provided a form of a social net for those who had nothing. An observant Jew at the time of Jesus who applied older stories to their lives would apply the story of Ruth and Boaz in Ruth 2:23. This provides an example how those who were poor gleaned in the harvest field; they did not become wealthy, but had enough to stay alive. The story illustrates how both foreigner and non-foreigner were entitled to Jewish protection as ethical treatment of people living in the same jurisdiction. The Jewish listeners to the Sermon on the Mount would have understood the peace sayings of Jesus through the concept of charity that provides for the support of those who lack the basics of life to survive. The call for social justice in the *Mishna* would have been in the minds of the listeners of the Sermon on the Mount.

2.6.4 Charity and Human Dignity

In order to understand the Jewish ethical understanding of the Sermon on the Mount, it is particularly important to examine the listener's perception of charity and dignity. This is done by looking at charity and dignity in the oral law. Charity and human dignity are vital for the human relationship. As discussed, the word *tzedakah* represents the charity of a person. In order to define *tzedakah, Bava Bathra* 9a, which was redacted in the same time and manner as *Pirkei Avot* the oral sayings of the rabbinical sages, defines how *tzedakah* was understood.[216] *Bava Bathra* 9a says, "charity is equal in importance to all the other

---

[216] Telushkin, *A Code of Jewish Ethics*, 156.

commandments combined."[217] This tradition originated from the writers of *Mishna* and *Talmud* who defined the ethics of Judaism.

The amount of charity a person provided for those less fortunate related to how human dignity is perceived. Human dignity was embodied in the values and *mitzvoth* in Judaism: "The concept of human dignity is well-ingrained throughout Judaism," writes Jacobs, "Those listening to the Sermon would identify the charitable acts of Jesus through such activities as feeding people, healing people, and listening to people. The book of Genesis describes human beings as created '*b'tzelem Elohim,*' in the image of God."[218] When an individual is charitable, that person is acting justly to those who have nothing or significantly less than the benefactor. Such giving is the litmus test of one's true sense of justice and right. This is evident in New Testament scholarship such as the Jewish book of Jude, which concludes its last verse by acknowledging the character of Jesus but recognizes that God is the one who is the source of the charity and power.[219]

2.6.5 Ethical Loans to be Interest-Free

Biblical rules for money lending represent the intent of a God who desires ethical, just givers in a community of believers. The listeners to the Sermon on the Mount would have understood that those who lend must not seek interest from fellow Jews.[220] The rules governing moneylending reveal more of the ethical dimension to community building. The Jewish moneylender could not lend money with interest to a fellow Jew; however, if the person was not a Jew, then one could charge interest.[221] There was a standard of care under

---

[217] Yasaif Asher Weiss, *Talmud* Bavli, 2nd ed., trans. Artscroll, (Brooklyn, New York: Mesorah, 2009), 95.

[218] Jacobs, *There Shall Be No Needy,* 12.

[219] DeSilva, *The Jewish Teachers of Jesus, James, and Jude*, 12.

[220] Worth, *The Sermon on the Mount,* 212.

which the Jewish believer was ethically bound toward the non-Jew in regards to moneylending. The Jewish believer could not take advantage of the non-Jew, even though they could charge interest. By removing the burden of interest on the principal of a loan to a fellow Jew, the stigma of borrowing money was diminished; thus, the lender and the borrower were on equal ground with each other. The biblical foundation comes from Proverbs 22:7 (NRSV), which states: "The rich rule over the poor, and the borrower is the slave of the lender." When a person lends money to another person, the reminder is that the loan is not 'their own' money; thus, one cannot take advantage of a brother because it would be using God's money to make money from their kindred. *Pirkei Avot* 2:14 quotes Rabbi Shimon, stating, "Every borrowing is borrowing from God, as it is said, 'the wicked one borrows and does not repay, but the righteous one is gracious and gives.'" *Pirkei Avot* quotes Psalm 37:21 (JPS): "The wicked man borrows and does not repay; the righteous is generous and keeps giving," which provides an ethical paradigm against failing to repay a loan. The listeners to the Sermon on the Mount would have understood this oral law defining ethical living for the Jewish believer. Jewish followers should treat fellow listeners of the Sermon on the Mount with dignity and respect.

2.7 **Conclusion**

Jewish ethical thought during the lifetime of Jesus would have greatly affected the reception and comprehension of Jesus' Sermon on the Mount. This chapter has explored key historical documents that give glimpses of the cultural and philosophical views of the age. The oral law, the Dead Sea Scrolls, and the pseudepigrapha provide a glimpse into the many and diverse views of Jewish believers at the time of Jesus. Biblical sources shed light upon ancient Jewish views of peace and a peaceful kingdom, including the awaited *moshiach* or

---

[221] Amy-Jill Levine and Marc Zvi Brettler, *The Jewish Annotated New Testament* (Oxford: Oxford University Press, 2011), 12.

messianic figure. Views of the *moshiach* figure were as varied as the different Jewish groups' expectation about a *moshiach*. The *moshiach* was identified as a spiritual leader by some Jewish groups and as a political leader by other Jewish groups, and sometimes both. The judicial system in biblical Judaism laid the foundation for Jewish ethics as regards political authority and violence. Since the oral law had a heavy influence upon Jewish thought at the start of the Common Era, *Pirkei Avot* is relevant as a primary ethical guide for Judaism. *Pirkei Avot* focuses on a variety of practical and relevant topics, such as the importance of seeking wisdom and counsel, distancing oneself from evildoers, loving peace and seeking non-confrontational solutions. As well, *Pirkei Avot* gives guidance regarding self-restraint, unselfish ethical service, respect, retributive justice, loving work and avoiding conflict. The *Avot* also provides commentary on communitarianism, submission to the oppressive rulers, as well as prayer for governmental welfare. In conjunction with these background sources, the Dead Sea Scrolls reveal another strand to the eschatological and political thought of the age.

The understanding of charity, or *tzedakah*, is also worthy of mention in the context of the ethics of the period. Jesus called on the listeners of his Sermon to be ethical through kindness and generosity in dealing with their neighbours. Loans with cloaks are to be just, charity was paramount, and a social gospel was reaffirmed with emphasis on *tzedakah*. Understanding the political and cultural climate and ethical structure of the age, as presented by these sources, the modern day reader is better equipped to unravel how the ancient audience may have understood the Sermon. Jesus' peace sayings and calls to non-violence are better grasped by taking into account the background context of the discourse and the prevailing perceptions of the day rooted in the domestic and foreign laws and codes of the era.

Having concluded a foundational discussion of the ethics and political understandings of the day, the actual Sermon itself may now be analysed with regards to Jesus' peace sayings and non-violence, allowing a more accurate understanding of what the audience may actually have heard, received and responded to.

CHAPTER 3

AN OUTLINE OF THE SERMON AND ITS PEACE SAYINGS

3.1 Introduction

The Sermon on the Mount has many different interpretations. Some scholars interpret the Sermon's Beatitudes as ethical demands that "people must actualise if they are to be admited to the yet-future kingdom of heaven," whilst others believe that the Sermon was a promise for an eschatological kingdom, especially when read in conjunction with the Beatitudes.[222] This dissertation focuses on the likely ethical understandings of the Sermon on the part of the listeners who heard Jesus.

This chapter has two sections. The first section focuses on the how the Sermon on the Mount came about. To understand the Sermon, the structure and writing style are examined in order demonstrate the correlation between the audience, the peace sayings, and how these sayings are presented. Also, this chapter utilizes other Jewish literature in order to compare the Sermon with other writings common at the time of Jesus. It will not examine all of the interpretations of the Sermon, but will provide a basic layout in order to examine its peace sayings. In no way does this necessarily discount the uniqueness of the message given by Jesus, but this chapter does set out how a unique *midrash* of Jesus bridges Jewish and Christian peace-sayings at his time.

The second section examines different peace sayings and character traits that precipitate peaceful actions from the Sermon on the Mount. The discussion of Matthew 5:5 will look at the concept of 'meekness' and examine its role in the character of a person. This is intrinsically tied to Matthew 5:9 with the term 'peacemaker'. The meekness of a person is

---

[222] Charles H. Talbert, *Reading the Sermon on the Mount* (Columbia, SC: University of South Carolina, 2004), 47.

part of being a peacemaker because of the value ethics associated with the term peacemaker. The value-ethics associated with being peaceful and happy (the term 'happy' will be defined) are part of the Sermon. These peace ethics are important to deciphering the Sermon's ideology. Chapter 3 continues with an examination of Matthew 5:38-42 in order to understand the roles that equality, love, and non-retaliation have in the peace sayings. Jesus does not condone an increase in violence but provides an alternative to violence, building on ideologies from the *Mishna* that create social equality between all people.

3.2 Composition of the Sermon

The Sermon on the Mount is found in Matthew 5-7. It has six antitheses which separate the Sermon into sections.

3.2.1 The Audience of the Sermon

This dissertation focuses on the Jewish audience at the Sermon on the Mount. It does not discount the idea that non-Jewish people were there, nor that the disciples were present too. However, it concurs with Saldarini that they were a group of Jews who believed in Jesus, still thought of themselves as Jews, and identified themselves as a Jewish community.[223]

3.2.1.1 *Jewish Listeners*

The style and composition of the Sermon on the Mount is Jewish.[224] It reflects writing geared to Jewish listeners from a Jewish authorship[225] and reveals a Jewish Jesus through the practices, ethical sayings, and peace sayings.[226] Jesus emerges from the text as a Jew who conforms to the religious practices of his nation; thus, he is aligned doctrinally with the body

---

[223] Saldarini, *Matthew's Christian-Jewish Community, 1-2.*

[224] Talbert, *Reading the Sermon on the Mount,* 3.

[225] Vermes, *The Religion of Jesus the Jew,* 20.

[226] Talbert, *Reading the Sermon on the Mount,* 3-4; Saldarini, *Matthew's Christian-Jewish Community,* 2.

of people who are listening to him.[227] The Sermon on the Mount addresses a Jewish Christian[228] audience, with a minority being gentile Christian.[229] Saldarini contends that the Sermon on the Mount in Matthew contains elements that vary from the Lukan account and that point to its Jewish authorship.[230] Pinchas Lapide argues that the writing style and composition of the Sermon in Matthew differ from the writing style of the rest of that gospel and that the Sermon differs in "Jesus' Jewishness and the fundamentally Hebraic quality of his glad tidings."[231] The writer of Matthew depicts a Jesus who in style, form, and content is very Jewish. The Sermon on the Mount is "characteristic of older scholarship... [and] individual elements of the Sermon on the Mount can be traced back to the historical Jesus."*[232]* The Sermon's Q source provides a common understanding of Jesus, although the Lukan Sermon on the Plain and Matthew's Sermon on the Mount vary in details.[233] The Sermon on the Mount appears in both Matthew and Luke with calls for love. The gospel of Mark may have been source of the Sermon; the Q sayings may be a primary source for the gospels of Matthew and Luke. Burridge contends that the peace sayings are part of the Q

---

[227] Vermes, *The Religion of Jesus the Jew,* 12.

[228] Jewish Christian adherents to Judaism were those who followed Torah completely but acknowledged Jesus (Yeshua) as the *moshiach.* This view creates a split between Rabbinic Judaism and Proto-orthodox Christianity. The traditional view has been that Judaism existed before Christianity and that Christianity separated from Judaism some time after the destruction of the Second Temple. Recent scholarship argues that there were many competing Jewish sects in Judea during Second Temple period and that what became Rabbinic Judaism and Proto-orthodox Christianity were but two of these. The Jewish Christian adherents would not have been different during the time of Jewish in the Jewish *halacha,* or observance of Jewish law.

[229] Senior, "Viewing the Jewish Jesus of History through the Lens of Matthew's Gospel," 82.

[230] Saldarini, *Matthew's Christian-Jewish Community,* 1-2.

[231] Pinchas Lapide, *The Sermon on the Mount* (New York: Orbis, 1986), 8.

[232] Betz, *Essays on the Sermon on the Mount,* 17.

[233] The Q source (also Q document, Q Gospel, Q Sayings Gospel, or Q) is a hypothetical collection of Jesus' sayings of Jesus, which may have been one of two written sources behind Matthew and Luke. Q (short for the German *Quelle,* or "source") is defined as the common material found in both Matthew and Luke but not in Mark. This collection was in the oral tradition of the Early Church and contains *logia* or quotations of Jesus; however, it has never been found and so remains a hypothesis. Identifying the Q source does not suggest that Jesus' sayings were not unique.

source and defines 'love your enemies' thus: "The centrality of love in Jesus' ethics even extends to the love of enemies. The Q-saying of Matt. 5:38-48/Luke 6:27-36 goes beyond mere non-retaliation to positive love for enemies."[234] This understanding of positive love connects in authorship and historical authorship to the Jewish understanding of the Sermon at the time of Jesus. Betz writes:

> The Matthean SM [Sermon on the Mount] is a source that has been transmitted intact and integrated by the evangelist into the composition of his Gospel but this source does not simply derive from the historical Jesus, in the sense that Jesus is the author of all the sayings in their present form and context. Rather, the SM represents a pre-Matthean composition of a redactional nature. Thus the methods of form and redaction criticism are to be further employed; it is only that they should not be applied to the Gospel as a whole, but merely the section Matt. 5:3-7:27.[235]

The Matthean Sermon does not prove that the Jesus sayings were spoken by Jesus, but indicate a commonality of sources between Luke and Matthew and an older source document known as Q. This older source document provides a basic understanding of both writers, who wrote the Sermon from a Jewish composition. The writers of the Synoptic Gospels were Jewish writers addressing a Jewish audience:

> According to numerous apologetic volumes, all the New Testament authors are Jewish: Paul is Jewish; Mark and Luke are Jewish; Matthew, John, the author of Hebrews, the Author of Revelation, all Jews. The argument also insists that these authors are writing mostly to Jews or at least to communities comprising Jews and Gentiles. Thus, the books of the New Testament cannot be anti-Jewish; on the contrary, they are as Jewish as can be.[236]

The Sermon on the Mount contains no conclusive evidence that it was composed after the Hellenization of the Jewish-Christian movement, when the Jewish-Christian movement

---

[234] Ibid.

[235] Ibid., 18-19.

[236] Levine, *The Misunderstood Jew,* 111.

became more Greek than Jewish and ultimately stopped functioning as a sect of Judaism. Indeed, there is no evidence in the synoptic Gospels that Jesus has a sense of mission to the Gentiles as an exclusive ministry.[237]

The Jewish listeners to the Sermon on the Mount would have understood the Sermon through their own Jewish lens and would have interpreted the theologies of Jesus through a native Jewish understanding, while the Gentile listeners would possibly have perceived it differently. The result is a Jewish Jesus talking to a Jewish audience mixed with Gentiles.

3.2.1.2 *The Sermon Addresses a Jewish Audience*

The religion of Jesus was authentically Jewish.[238] Those who heard Jesus speak were in the student role, affirming Jesus as a teacher (Matthew 7:28). Saldarini points out that the writings in Matthew "had close relations with the Jewish community."[239] Some writers assert that Jesus intended these teachings for his twelve disciples only and that applying the Sermon beyond them is not appropriate. For example, Kennedy says, "To whom did Jesus address the teachings of the Sermon? It has been assumed by some commentators, at least since the time of John Chrysostom (c. 347-407), that the sermon is primarily addressed to the disciples and only secondarily to others."[240] The disciples were Jewish; thus, even if the audience was only the disciples, the audience would still have been Jewish. Whether the Sermon was to the disciples who would have repeated the information to the rest of the Jewish world or to all people at the time of Jesus does not alter its Jewish nature. Other authors concur with it being a Jewish audience. Davis supports this, but limits the argument by indicating that the Sermon

---

[237] Bernard J. Lee, *The Galilean Jewishness of Jesus* (New York: Paulist, 1988), 67.

[238] Vermes, *The Religion of Jesus the Jew*, 184.

[239] Saldarini, *Matthew's Christian-Jewish Community,* 2.

[240] George Kennedy, *New Testament Interpretation Through Rhetorical Criticism* (Chapel Hill, NC: University of North Carolina Press, 1984), 40.

does not address institutional politics, such as a court system, but the disciples themselves: "It is important to remember that Jesus is addressing the disciples and not the Jewish court system. Jesus is addressing offending situations from the perspective of the offended, while the law addresses it from the perspective of the offender."[241]

Whether one sees the intended audience of the Sermon as the disciples or as another body of people rests largely on the referent of the word 'them' *(autous)* in Matt 5:2 (NRSV), which states, "And he opened his mouth and taught them." It may represent all of those in attendance; however, Kennedy suggests that the text is ambiguous in this regard:

> The textual basis for this conclusion is the 'them' (autous) of 5:2, for which the closest grammatical antecedent is the 'disciples' of 5:1. But this interpretation must be set against the 'them' of 7:28 in the closure of the speech, 'for he taught *them* [emphasis added] as one having authority,' where 'them' grammatically can only refer to the crowd as a whole. 'Them' in 5:2 can in fact also refer to the crowd, which is mentioned in 5:1. This interpretation is confirmed by 7:24, 'everyone then who hears these words.' That the entire crowd constitutes the audience is further supported by the various categories of people mentioned in the Beatitudes and throughout: the poor, the grief-stricken, the meek, those contemplating divorce, all Jews who will pray.[242]

In the Sermon, Jesus is addressing a group or crowd of people who are mostly Jewish. He seems to address all people who are in need of healing, who are suffering, and who are not privileged. Jesus was elaborating on Jewish ethical obligations towards those who are in need of restitution. His Sermon applies to people contemplating divorce (Matthew 5:31), people who pray (Matthew 6:5-6,9), and those in need (Matthew 6:8,32). The Jewish audience

---

[241] Davis, *Lex Talionis in Early Judaism*, 167.

[242] Kennedy, *New Testament Interpretation*, 40.

would have understood that the teachings in the Sermon on the Mount represent an "ethical advance" on the *lex talionis*.[243]

3.2.1.3 *The Jewish Kingdom and Gentile Converts*

The Sermon on the Mount probably addressed both Jews and Gentiles, since non-Jews did convert to Judaism. The figure of a *moshiach* stabilizes peace between Jews and Gentiles. Saldarini contends that the Sermon on the Mount envisions "his group attracting gentiles to Israel. In this hope, he is at one with many parts of the Jewish community which received converts and welcomed gentiles to synagogue services and instructions."[244] The writer of the Sermon divides it into six antitheses: "The six so-called antitheses (5:21-48) are not understood by Matthew as changes in God's law, but as a more penetrating appreciation of and obedience to the law. The actions encouraged are not violations of any biblical law; they uphold the law."[245] Torah observance for the Jew creates the Jewish identity of a person.[246]

3.2.2 The Sermon on the Mount and Jewish Wisdom Literature

The influence of Jewish wisdom literature on the Sermon on the Mount is reflected in the writing styles. Wisdom literature departs from early Hebraic texts that tell of the decrees of God through prophets and kings, and instead acknowledges the plethora of human emotions in daily life, while recommending how humans can maintain a relationship with God. The form, style, and content of the Jewish wisdom writings are all reflected in the Sermon on the Mount in the Matthean version. Betz writes:

> Those comparative texts standing nearest literally to the SM [Sermon on the Mount] are, in the first instance, those which belong to the Jewish Wisdom tradition. *Pirkei*

---

[243] Davis, *Lex Talionis in Early Judaism*, 167.

[244] Saldarini, *Matthew's Christian-Jewish Community,* 200.

[245] Ibid., 162.

[246] Ibid.

Avot, with its commentary *Avot de Rabbi Natan*, and so-called *Manual of Discipline* from Qumran are formally related, though they derive from other Jewish movements.[247]

The writing structure of the *Avot* demonstrates a structure similar to the writing of the Sermon on the Mount, even though the movements which they arose from may be different. *Pirkei Avot* provides peace sayings similar to the Sermon. "These sayings and teachings of the then-contemporary rabbis provide significant parallels to the moral message of Jesus' Sermon on the Mount."[248] The *Avot* provides a moral message to its readers just as Jesus' Sermon on the Mount provides a similar message to the Jewish audience.

3.2.3 The Structure of the Sermon

The Sermon on the Mount starts with the Beatitudes.[249] The beatitudes establish the themes of the Sermon on the Mount: poverty, hunger, persecution, dependence on God, nonaggression, and non-retaliation.[250] The Sermon is structured to provide discussion of each of these ethical actions, and the Beatitude provides a poltical solution by providing hope in the Kingdom of Heaven. Thus, both examples of suffering and responses to such suffering are covered in the Sermon on the Mount. Following the Beatitudes are 6 antitheses in verses 17-48 of the Sermon on the Mount, which are teachings expanding the Mosaic law. These six antitheses address (a) fulfillment of the Law, (b) murder, (c) adultery, (d) divorce, (e) oaths, (f) "an eye for an eye", and (g) love your enemies. Hays describes the antitheses as intensification of the law: "in most of the six antitheses, the teaching of Jesus constitutes an intensification – rather than an abrogation – of the requirements of the Law. The Law

---

[247] Betz, *Essays on the Sermon on the Mount*, 22.

[248] Brad H. Young, *Meet the Rabbis* (Peabody, MA: Hendrickson, 2007), 120.

[249] Anna Wierzbicka, *What Did Jesus Mean? Explaining the Sermon on the Mount and the Parables in Simple and Universal Human Concepts* (Oxford: Oxford University Press, 2001), 29.

[250] Ibid.

prohibits murder, but Jesus forbids even anger; the Law prohibits adultery, but Jesus forbids even lust."[251] Such simplicity in organization works to emphasise each antithesis. These six antitheses expound existing Mosaic law that was prevalent in the time of Jesus; thus, the listener to the Sermon on the Mount probably had a working knowledge of the subject matter of them, even if they were not categorised into six antitheses. A gentile may not have been so certain to understand the structure; however, the structure of the Sermon provides a unique view of Jesus' application of Mosaic law.

3.2.4 The Sermon on the Mount's Focus on Ethical Sayings

The Sermon on the Mount preaches about the poor and hungry. Listeners would have heard ethical sayings teaching care and protection through a social gospel. Caring for people who are less privileged is presented as ethically important. Wylen points out that "when Jesus speaks to the crowds, the gospel report is that they come away amazed. And see what amazes them! (Matt 7:28-29). What may have been most amazing was not the content of the Sermon on the Mount, which is in line with typical Jewish ethics and such teaching."[252] The contents of the Sermon is traditional Jewish sayings, and even the peace sayings are reflective of the ethical thought of the day. The crowds who listened to Jesus were amazed not only because of Jesus' unique grasp and *midrash* style, but by the manner in which he combined with his words, charity, compassion, and restoration of people.

3.2.5 Matthew 5:5 and Meekness

The Sermon on the Mount praises the ethical virtue of meekness in Matt 5:5. Restraint is paramount in Matthew 5:5 (NRSV), which states, "Blessed are the meek, for they will inherit the earth." The extent to which meekness influences the ethical sayings of Jesus determines

---

[251] Richard B. Hays, *The Moral Vision of the New Testament,* (San Francisco: Harper Collins, 1996), 324.

[252] Stephen M. Wylen, *The Jews in the Time of Jesus,* (New York: Paulist, 1996), 164.

whether Jesus was providing a unique theological change to Jewish intellectual thought. Lachs contends that the discussion of *meekness* is a scribal addition.[253] The Lukan account of the Sermon on the Mount is known as the Sermon on the Plain.[254] The Sermon on the Plain does not have this discussion of meekness. How one defines meekness influences how one applies the Sermon on the Mount to their life. To a Jew at the time of Jesus, meekness carried a different meaning.

This ethical value carries an eschatological impact, as followers embodying meekness will inherit the earth in Matthew 5:5, because how one inherits the earth is subject to the many different views of Judaism at the time. In both the Hebrew Bible and the *midrash*, the meek are those who are just in their actions. The meek are "people who do not take advantage of their position." (Ps 37:11; Prov 16:19; b Shabb. 30b; b Ned. 38a).[255] Other interpretations of meekness see it as akin to humility: "Wherever the Greek word (here translated as 'meek,' or better, humble), occurs in the Bible, it always points to peacefulness or peacemaking."[256] The term 'meek' implies peace and peacefulness, as well as gentleness and lowliness. The Greek word *preus (praeis)* is found in Matthew 5:5 as well as Matthew 11:29, 21:5, and 1 Peter 3:4 and has the meaning of 'meek'; however, this difficult-to-translate root (*pra-*) means *more than* that. *Biblical* meekness is *not weakness* but rather refers to exercising *God's strength* under *his control* – i.e. demonstrating power without undue harshness.[257]

The understanding of the text sheds light upon the Sermon on the Mount as meekness and peacemaking are both important. The image portrayed to the listeners to the Sermon on the

---

[253] Lachs, *A Rabbinic Commentary on the New Testament*, 69.

[254] In Christianity, the Sermon on the Plain refers to a set of teachings by Jesus in the Gospel of Luke, in 6:17-49. This sermon may be compared to the longer Sermon on the Mount in the Gospel of Matthew.

[255] Levine and Brettler, *The Jewish Annotated New Testament*, 8.

[256] Glen H. Stassen and David P. Gushee, *Kingdom Ethics,* (Downers Grove, IL: Intervarsity, 2003), 40.

[257] James Strong, *Strong's Exhaustive Concordance of the Bible,* (Nashville, TN: Royal, 2010), 60.

Mount is that of a meek person who does not take advantage of their position; thus, they are a meek person who inherits the earth. This understanding of the text provides a stark contrast to a militant Zealot faction as well as a militarised *moshiach*.

3.2.5.1 *Matthew 5:9 and Peacemakers*

In the Sermon on the Mount, 'peacemaker' describes a role Jesus reconnects to the listener. Matthew 5:9 states: "Blessed are the peacemakers, for they will be called children of God." Lachs contends that the meaning of the word is unclear because it is an adjective referring both to those who make peace and those who are peaceful.[258] Relevant to an understanding of the peace sayings is the correlation between Matthew 5:9 and the *Mishna.* Since the word "blessed" may be better translated as "happy," the text may better read "happy are those peacemakers" or "happy are the peaceful."[259,260] The discussion of 'peacemaker' in Matthew 5:9 overlaps with the oral law in *b. Ber. 64a* and *Pesiq. Rav Kah 18:6-9.*[261] It presents the ethical attributes of peace in daily living as a Jewish person. Peacemakers are also known as *children of God* because they exhibit character attributes of God. Furthermore, Lachs contends that verses 7-9 deal with the unfortunates of society.[262]

The Lukan version of the Sermon on the Plain has a different intent than the Matthean version. Luke 6:22-23 (NRSV) states: "Blessed are you when people hate you, and when they exclude you, revile you, and defame you on account of the Son of Man. Rejoice in that day and leap for joy, for surely your reward is great in heaven; for that is what their ancestors did to the prophets." Being called children of God is Matthew's highest accolade while Luke promises instead a reward great in heaven; to Lachs, this points to the social differences of

---

[258] Ibid.

[259] Ibid.

[260] Levine and Brettler. *The Jewish Annotated New Testament,* 10.

[261] Ibid.

[262] Lachs, *A Rabbinic Commentary on the New Testament,* 77.

the writers.[263] Lach contends that the language used in Matthew's version reflects a community that has been rejected.[264]

The writer of Matthew focuses on a Jewish Christian minority in distress.[265] In order to understand the ethical and political nature of a peacemaker, it is important to understand the interpretation of 'blessed' in the Beatitudes in the Matthew context. How one translates the word 'blessed' impacts on how the text peacemaker is received. Lachs contends that it is translated as 'happy.'[266] Other translations suggest that it refers to being a privileged recipient of divine favour, or that the person so described is 'fortunate.' Using the translation of the term 'fortunate' are the peacemakers, for they will be called children of God, the reverse of 'fortunate' implies that those who do not seek peace are unfortunate. Vermes contends that the peacemakers are synonymous with children of God. Those "who imitate the heavenly source of shalom, can successfully strive for peace on earth and deserve to be called sons of God."[267] Consequently, those who are peacemakers are fortunate. Stassen and Gushee write:

> Peacemaker … is the right translation… for a positive action, reconciliation, is envisioned: the peacemakers seek to bring about peace. Since the previous Beatitudes concern social relations, surely the meaning here is social, not simply peace between individuals and God, as is frequently claimed.[268]

The peacemaker is not someone who solely seeks to have peace with God but who lives an ethical life seeking peace socially in the present world, the *Kingdom of Heaven*, as seen throughout the New Testament gospels. The listener to the Sermon on the Mount would

---

[263] Lachs, *A Rabbinic Commentary on the New Testament*, 77.

[264] Ibid.

[265] Senior, "Viewing the Jewish Jesus of History through the Lens of Matthew's Gospel," 82.

[266] Lachs, *A Rabbinic Commentary on the New Testament*, 76.

[267] Vermes, *The Religion of Jesus the Jew,* 157.

[268] Stassen and Gushee, *Kingdom Ethics*, 45.

understand that it positioned peace sayings in the intellectual thought of Judaism at the time of Jesus.

3.2.6 Matthew 5:39 and Resisting

Whether peace is to be promoted through resisting or not resisting is an issue that has led to many different interpretations that have shaped Christian thought.[269] Matthew 5:39 (NRSV) states that a prohibition exists regarding 'resisting' an evildoer; instead, he advocates turning the cheek towards an aggressor, stating: "but I say to you, do not resist an evildoer…if anyone strikes you on the right cheek, turn the other also." The term 'resist' is sometimes interpreted as retaliatory action with the intent of revenge. Stansen and Gushee interpret it as meaning "but I say to you, do not retaliate revengefully by evil means." The authors point out that the verse is "not an imperative in the Greek, but an infinitive— probably with implied imperatival meaning" (in koine Greek, the imperative may be used when commanding or requesting).[270] The text implies 'resisting' as including those actions that result in insult because there is an intent of revenge in the action.[271]

The Greek word *antistēnai* occurs fourteen times in the New Testament. There are three translations of the word according to Davis: "(1) resistance, (2) retaliation, (3) violent rebellion or even armed revolt."[272] By not 'resisting' an evildoer, "the subject here seems to be the insult (shame), not physical injury."[273] Therefore an individual is able to shame an evildoer because of the actions they are doing. This is very different to being a doormat for those who commit evil.

---

[269] *See* J. H. Yoder, *Christian Attitudes to War, Peace, and Revolution* (Grand Rapids, Michigan: Brazos Press, 2009).

[270] Stansen and Gushee, *Kingdom Ethics*, 137.

[271] Ibid.

[272] Davis, *Lex Talionis in Early Judaism*, 105.

[273] Lachs, *A Rabbinic Commentary on the New Testament*, 104.

The Matthean version of the Sermon varies from the Lukan Sermon on the Plain, which states, "to him who strikes you on the cheek, offer the other also" (Luke 6:29 NRSV). Matthew's account uses the term *antistēnai,* while the Lukan account focuses on turning the cheek. The ethical implication of resisting by turning the right check implies more than being slapped; the "right cheek presumes a back-handed slap. Turn the other, respond with neither violence nor abjection."[274] The ethical peace saying in Matthew 5:39 implies more than suffering but calls for peace through alternative means.

3.2.6.1 *Resistance and its Connection with the Lex Talionis*

Matthew 5:39 is connected to Matthew 5:38. The *lex talionis* in Matthew 5:38-42 provides an understanding of Jewish thought because non-violent action would go hand in hand with *lex talionis.*[275] David Stern suggests that the *lex talionis* suggests a connection between the audience of the Sermon of the Mount and the intent of the text,[276] which correlates with the oral law found in the *midrash.* The connection between the *Bava Kama* 8:1 in the *Midrash* and the peace sayings of the Sermon on the Mount show a commonality between a compassionate ethical person and the responsibilities Jesus discusses in the Sermon on the Mount. *Bava Kama* 8:1 states:

One who wounds his neighbor is liable to pay the following five things: damage, pain, healing, loss of time, and disgrace. "Damage." – If he blinds one's eye, cuts off his hand, or breaks his leg, the injured person is considered as if he were a slave sold in the market, and he is appraised at his former and his present value. "Pain." – If he burns him with a

---

[274] Levine and Brettler, *The Jewish Annotated New Testament,* 12.

[275] James G. Crossley, "Book Review of *Lex Talionis in Early Judaism and the Exhortation of Jesus in Matthew 5:38-42,*" *Journal for the Study of the New Testament* 26, no. 1 (2006), 50.

[276] David H. Stern, *Jewish New Testament Commentary* (Clarksville, MD: Jewish New Testament, 1992), 29.

spit or with a nail, if even only on the nail (of his hand or foot), where it produces no wound, it is appraised how much a man his equal would take to suffer such pain. "Healing." – If he caused him bodily injury, he must heal him; if pus collected by reason of the wound, he must cause him to be healed; if, however, not by reason of the wound, he is free. If the wound heals up and breaks out again, even several times, he must cause it to be healed; if, however, it once heals up thoroughly, he is no more obliged to heal it. "Loss of time." – The injured person is considered as if he were a watchman of a pumpkin field, as he was already paid the value of his hand or foot. The disgrace is appraised with consideration of the station and rank of the one who causes as well as of the one who suffers it.[277]

Bava Kama 8:1 stipulates the ethical ways in which a Jewish person is required to compensate a person for wrongdoing in damages, pain, healing, loss of time, and disgrace. The *Mishna* teaches how a compassionate person should act non-violently to help a person who has been wronged. Stern goes so far as to claim that the peace and ethical sayings reveal that "Judaism and New Testament religion are really the same."[278,279] The intellectual foundation that forms both religions are similar in thought, which helps with deciphering the New Testament; however, Judaism and Christianity became different religions.[280] The connection between the application of *lex talionis* in *Bava Kama* 8:1 and the intent of Jesus in Matthew 5:38-42 illustrates a Jewish understanding of compassionate actions.

In contrast to Stern, Vermes describes retaliation in Matthew 5:38-42 as "hyperbolical" and states that the text is a "disavowal of vindictiveness" in the *lex talionis* because it

---

[277] *Bava Kama* 8:1.

[278] Ibid., 31.

[279] David Fox Sandmel, "The Christian Reclamation of Judaism," *Judaism: A Quarterly Journal of Jewish Life and Thought*, volume 54, numbers 3/4 (2005), 251-63.

[280] Ibid.

removes retaliation through vindictive measures from individual discretionary action.[281]
According to Vermes, the text found in Matthew 5:38-42 is a supererogation of our ethical
responsibilities to others.[282]

3.2.6.2 *Doctrine of Restraint Connects with Judicial Setting*

The doctrine of restraint in connection with non-violence was connected to the judicial
system at the time of Jesus. When the judicial system has been misapplied, it can create an
imbalance of justice for the parties involved. Worth contends that restraint when applied to a
judicial system limits such an imbalance of power.[283] The doctrine of restraint balances justice
between parties by creating a protection for a person who is subject to the *lex talionis,* but
Jesus' sayings in verse 39 extend beyond *lex talionis.* An accused person should not escalate
a lawsuit and should not run away from it either.[284] The role that the doctrine of restraint plays
in the Sermon limits how much power and force are applied to creating peace.

3.2.6.3 *Job 16:10 and Influence on Non-Retaliation*

Job 16:10 contains an important treatment of the issue of striking in the Hebrew Scriptures.
It describes the treatment received by Job during his period of torment: "They have gaped at
me with their mouths; they have struck me insolently on the cheek; they mass themselves
together against me." This is similar to the way Jesus suffered physical insults without
retaliating against his aggressors.[285] The Sermon on the Mount and the Job story each
demonstrate "an insulting action."[286] Edgar Gibson argues that smiting someone on the cheek

---

[281] Vermes, *The Religion of Jesus the Jew,* 35.

[282] Ibid., 36.

[283] Ibid.

[284] Ibid., 236-237.

[285] Ibid., 246.

was a common means of insult, which is in line with the Job story.[287] The similarity between what the Sermon's Jesus says and Job being smitten on the cheek show a commonality for insulting a person.

3.2.6.4 *The Influence of Lamentations 3:25-30 on Non-Retaliation*

Lamentations 3:25-30 is often overlooked when interpreting Matt 5:39 under the assumption that Jesus presented new theology and political ideology.[288] Lamentations 3:28-30 (JPS) reads: "Let him sit alone and be patient, When he has laid it upon him. Let him put his mouth to the dust—There may yet be hope. Let him offer his cheek to the smiter; let him be surfeited with mockery." Lamentations 2:25-30 teaches patience that the waiting one has for God's compassion and mercy. It is not about "swallow[ing] insults without retaliating", but about having patience in one's reaction.[289] The insults may not be specifically physical in nature, and the conclusion drawn by Worth is that "Jesus did not originate some new doctrine in his teaching on nonretaliation, but was faithfully presenting an approach voiced by the sages recorded in the Old Testament."[290] An insult does not have to be physical, but may consist of verbal, social, economic, or even religious attacks on a person. In regards to Matthew 5:39 and the peace sayings, a person does not have to attack another person to hurt them - they can oppress them in other ways.

---

[286] Victor E. Reichart, *Job: With Hebrew Text and English Translation* (Hindhead, Surrey, UK: Soncino, 1946), 82.

[287] Edgar C.S. Gibson, *Book of Job,* Westminster Commentary Series, (Greenwood, SC: Attic, 1976), 119.

[288] Ibid., 249-50.

[289] Norman C. Habel, *Jeremiah/ Lamentations,* Concordia Commentary (St.Louis, MO: Concordia, 1968), 407.

[290] Worth, *The Sermon on the Mount,* 252.

3.2.6.5 *Isaiah 50:6 and its Influence on Non-Retaliation*

Isaiah 50:6 discusses how a person responds to violence. According to Worth, the Jews

would have been aware of the Isaiah 50:6 text. Isaiah 50:6 (JPS) states: "I offered my back to

the floggers, and my cheeks to those who tore out my hair. I did not hide my face from insult

and spittle." The author of Matthew 5:39 may have extend his understanding of Isaiah 50:6 to

another person who strikes on the cheek, as seen in the Sermon on the Mount.[291] Worth

contends that there is a link between the word 'cheek' in the Sermon, in Exodus 21:24, and in

Isaiah 50:6 because of the allusion to a messianic kingdom.[292] M.D. Goulder indicates that

those verbal links are "too strong to be accidental: the *'but I say to you'* section is a *midrashic*

expansion of Isaiah" because they all discuss the role of violence and the reaction a person

has towards the person who committed violence.[293] The commentary provided by Jesus is not

new, but an expository or *midrashic* commentary on an existing Exodus text.[294]

Isaiah 50 has many parallels with the sayings of Jesus in the Sermon on the Mount, such

as Isaiah 50:1 (JPS) in which a discussion of a bill of divorce occurs and creditors, as well as

Isaiah 50:6 (JPS) in which the person being flogged turns their cheek. Jesus uses *haftorah* in

the Sermon on the Mount, which is reading from the Prophets after reading Torah.[295] Jesus is

using Isaiah 50 and drawing a similarity with the Sermon on the Mount. This similarity in

---

[291] Ibid., 253.

[292] Ibid., 253.

[293] M. D. Goulder, *Midrash and Lection in Matthew* (London: SPCK, 1977), 293.

[294] The period in which Isaiah 50:6 is written is known as the Deutero-Isaiah period. Deutero-Isaiah (chapters 40–55) is the work of a 6th-century BCE author writing near the end of the Babylonian captivity.

[295] *Haftorah* became in use after 168 BCE, but no one knows for certain its origins. The most common explanation, accepted by some traditional Jewish authorities, is that in 168 BCE, when the Jews were under the rule of the Seleucid king Antiochus IV Epiphanes, they were forbidden from reading the Torah and made do with a substitute. When they were again able to read the Torah, they kept reading the *haftorah* as well. This practice continued through the Second Temple period and after the fall of the Second Temple. Certainly the *haftorah* was read, although it was not compulsory, by at least 70 CE because the Talmud mentions that a *haftorah* was read in the presence of Rabbi Eliezer ben Hyrcanus.

Matthew 5:39 is earlier at 31-32 (NRSV): "It was also said, 'whoever divorces his wife, let him give her a certificate of divorce.' But I say to you that anyone who divorces his wife, except on the ground of unchastity, causes her to commit adultery; and whoever marries a divorced woman commits adultery." This text has engendered much debate. Comparison between this version on the Sermon and the layout and content of Isaiah 50 (JPS) reveals similarity between Isaiah 50:1 (JPS) and the way in which his disciples are to follow Jesus in the Sermon on the Mount. Furthermore, Isaiah 51:1 (JPS) explains that those who follow God pursue justice. In both chapters of Isaiah, there is discussion of divorce and the role of the creditor. Isaiah 50:1 (JPS) states, "Thus says the Lord: 'Where is your mother's bill of divorce with which I put her away?'" Even if this verse is understood as symbolic of the covenant between God and Israel being broken, it utilizes the metaphor of divorce which is also found in the Sermon on the Mount. Isaiah 50:1 (JPS) discusses creditors, "Or which of my creditors is it to whom I have sold you? No, because of your sins you were sold, and for your transgressions your mother was put away" is similar to Matthew 5:40 (which will be explored further later) which states, "and if anyone wants to sue you and take your coat, give your cloak as well." The Sermon demonstrates, not a new ethical paradigm foreign to its Jewish listeners, but consistency with Isaiah as regards the relationship between those in authority and those who are in submission to others.[296] The similarity of thought in Isaiah and Jesus' Sermon shows continuity and not a new doctrine.[297] The distinctiveness of sayings of Jesus lies in the connection they provide between Isaiah and the contemporary Jew of the time living under Roman rule.

3.2.7 Matthew 5:40 and Equality

---

[296] Worth, *The Sermon on the Mount,* 253.

[297] Warren Carter, *Matthew and Empire* (Harrisburg, PA: Trinity Press, 2001), 32.

Inequality between people can breed hostility. Matthew 5:40 looks beyond the concept of charity to the equality under law during the time of Jesus. The mode of keeping justice equalises people's rights. The text of Matthew 5:40 (NRSV) states: "and if anyone wants to sue you and take your coat, give your cloak as well." The text utilizes both the letter of the law and the spirit of the law through giving one's cloak as well. The text needs further clarification about the purpose for which the cloak being given—is this a legal action, or is this a new ethical saying by Jesus? The action described in Matthew is different in intent from the Lukan version, because in Luke 6:29 (NRSV), the text states that "If anyone strikes you on the cheek, offer the other also; and from anyone who takes away your coat do not withhold even your shirt." The Lukan account focuses less on legal action and more on the person's individual accountability for taking a cloak. In Matthew, a person may be sued for their cloak; however, in Luke, the action is someone taking the coat, whether legal or not. Lachs proposes that "here it is clearly a legal action in tort or contract which is described."[298] As outlined in Chapter 2, if a person used their cloak as collateral for a loan, then the person who lent them the money had restrictions on regress and risked public exposure if he took more than the required collateral. Only the poorest person would offer their clothes as collateral, because "most people owned only two garments; to strip naked would uncover the judiciary injustice."[299] If a person gave their undergarment as collateral and repay with excess from a judicial decision, then the court is publicly held accountable for enforcing the law.[300] The shaming of the oppressor by exposing their violation of Mosaic law leads society to see that the oppressor is not to be trusted. It is a non-violent form of passive-aggressive retaliation.

---

[298] Lachs, *A Rabbinic Commentary on the New Testament*, 104.

[299] Levine and Brettler, *The Jewish Annotated New Testament*, 12.

[300] Ibid.

The Sermon demonstrates how the listener who is subject to Roman authority in the political state also complied with Mosaic law. The audience of the Sermon on the Mount would have balanced the biblical laws of legal equality, knowing that they could not demand interest from fellow believers. Jesus' words are not new material; the listeners to the Sermon on the Mount understand that the ethical requirement to have equality with all people when they were arrears in debt, facing collection. Under the Roman rule, Jewish law was still practiced in the *Bet Dien*, which was typified in the Jesus crucifixion story. As well, the Jewish people who listened to the Sermon on the Mount would understand that shaming an oppressor was a form of non-violent assertion.

3.2.8 Matthew 5:41 and Oppression of the State

The sayings found in Matthew 5:41 are appropriate to the climate of the Sermon on the Mount and the ethics of the people who listened to it. Going the 'extra mile' has moulded and shaped the perception of Christian character for many generations; however, to understand what the listeners to the Sermon on the Mount most likely understood, one must look at the text with historical understanding. According to Davis, "it is clear that Old Testament *Lex Talionis* was to be implemented on a societal and governmental level in a judicial process for the nation of Israel." *Lex talionis* in Matthew 5:41 does not extend beyond the direct community of listeners: "Certainly it is addressed to the community of disciples but only from the perspective of the victim or person offended... It is not directed specifically to the government, courts or judges on how to punish offenders or carry out law on a societal level."[301] The behaviour that the Sermon on the Mount affirms is intended for the commonplace citizenry, not for legislators or governmental leadership on a national level because it was an occupied country.

---

[301] Davis, *Lex Talionis in Early Judaism*, 138.

The text of Matthew 5:41 (NRSV) states, "and if anyone forces you to go one mile, go also the second mile." The text is sometimes interpreted as an invitation to self-sacrifice. Others see the implications of nonviolent resistance to an oppressive state. In the time of Jesus, "Roman soldiers could conscript locals to carry their gear for one mile; going the second is nonviolent resistance."[302] The limitation on the amount of work ('work' included carrying the soldier's goods while walking with him) was limited to one mile by Roman law. "It literally means one thousand paces, but became a fixed length of eight stades – 4,454 feet = 1478 meters."[303] Levine and Brettler suggest that by volunteering to go a second mile, one would make the soldier lose control of the situation, which would unbalance the degree of power the soldier had over the servant.[304] It could also bring suspicion upon the soldier for conscripting a servant to carry a military pack in excess of the distance limited by law. The soldier could be subject to penalty for such a breach of protocol.[305] This would make a soldier think twice before employing the common folk (namely Jews), as it could end awkwardly for him. David Stern contends that this verse reflects Matthew 5:16, which maintains that actions are the light which reflects the character of a person.[306] Davis, on the other hand, asserts that Jesus does not give the option for a person to go only one mile or less; a literal reading of the text indicates, "Jesus recommends… with the present active imperative to go with him two."[307]

---

[302] Levine and Brettler, *The Jewish Annotated New Testament*, 12.

[303] Davis, *Lex Talionis in Early Judaism*, 145.

[304] Levine and Brettler, *The Jewish Annotated New Testament*, 12.

[305] Ibid.

[306] Stern, *Jewish New Testament Commentary*, 29.

[307] Davis, *Lex Talionis in Early Judaism*, 145.

Lachs proposes that the service a Roman soldier could require is "any impressed service."[308] Conversely, other scholars indicate that the 'carry his pack a second mile' reference in Matthew 5:41 is about loving your enemy when the enemy is, in actuality, the state itself. Stassen and Gushee suggest that "In fact, this specific rule—carry his pack a second mile—is one concrete expression of the general principle 'love your enemy.' (And the spirit in which one carried that pack a second mile would reflect quite clearly the extent to which the principle of the enemy –love was being demonstrated)."[309] How one carries a pack and walks the second mile, both literally and proverbially, defines the non-violent protest in the context of love. The listeners to the Sermon on the Mount would have balanced non-violent protest against genuine love and the need to submit to the state. The Sermon on the Mount would lead those listening to be obedient to the state by carrying a pack one mile while at the same time seeking justice through peaceful and ethical means and going a second.

3.2.9 Matthew 5:43-48 and Loving Enemies

The sixth antithesis of the Sermon on the Mount is about loving enemies, and it follows a traditional antithetical rhythm in design and content, such as is seen in other Jewish writings of the time.[310] The context of love defines the Sermon on the Mount in Matthew 5:43-48. The peace sayings found there characterise the acts of loving your 'neighbour' and loving your 'enemy' both as good behaviour and as a requirement of the general ethics promoted by Jesus. Matthew 5:43 (NRSV) states, "You have heard that it was said, 'you shall love your neighbour and hate your enemy,' but I say to you, love your enemies and pray for those who persecute you." The scripture referenced is Leviticus 19:18 (NRSV) "You shall not take vengeance or bear a grudge against any of your people, but you shall love your neighbour as

---

[308] Lachs, *A Rabbinic Commentary on the New Testament*, 105.

[309] Stassen and Gushee, *Kingdom Ethics*, 102-03.

[310] Goulder, *Midrash and Lection in Matthew*, 294.

yourself: I am the Lord." David Stern translates Matthew 5:43 under the influence of oral law as, "You have heard that our fathers were told 'love your neighbor' and hate your enemy."[311] Stern's translation leans on the oral tradition as the source of Jesus' version of the peace sayings. This peace saying in the Sermon on the Mount makes reference to hating an enemy, but there is no record of this in the Hebrew Bible.

A text found at Qumran 1QS 9.21 discusses love and hatred in connection to one's enemy. 1QS 9-10 demonstrates the closest connection between loving the Sons of Light and hating the Sons of Darkness. There is no evidence to establish whether this was what Jesus was referring to.

Matthew 5:44-8 models love and prayer for enemies. The use of the term, 'Gentile' in this text indicates that the audience of the sermon was Jewish: the term 'Gentile' occurs only five times in the New Testament, three in Matthew (5.47, 6.7, 18.17), once in Galatians 2.14, and once in 3 John 7. It has been variously translated as 'Gentiles,' 'pagans,' and/or 'heathens'.[312] To love someone different, including Gentiles, is exemplified in the text by loving and praying for those who persecute you. The method of loving your enemy models rabbinical teachings:

> It is possible to see Jesus' command to 'love your enemies' as belonging to the same tradition as Rabbi Judah's ruling. Therefore, when Jesus states, according to Matthew 5:43, 'you have heard that it was said, you shall love your neighbor and hate your enemy,' he is not referring to a Pharisaic or proto-rabbinic view. More likely, he is referring to the composers of certain Dead Sea Scrolls, such as the Community Rule,

---

[311] Stern, *Jewish New Testament Commentary*, 1229.

[312] Lachs, *A Rabbinic Commentary on the New Testament*, 109.

who divide the world into those who follow 'the path for the wise' and therefore merit love and those other 'men of the pit' who deserve eternal hatred (1Qs9.21).[313]

Jesus' love sayings follow pre-existing sayings within various Jewish writings. Jesus often recalled people back to their own knowledge banks, referring to what they already knew or what was already known. David Stern contends that to 'love your enemies' subsequently became *midrash* and parallels *Orchot Tzaddikim* 15c.[314,315]

During the time of Jesus, "Jews were not to mistreat enemies (Proverbs 24.17; 25.21; Josephus, *ag.Ap.2.211*)."[316] Of all the behaviour required by Judaism in the time of Jesus, the most important, as seen in Matthew 22:37-39 was to treat others with dignity and respect.[317] Matthew 5:44-8 (NRSV) reflects this:

> Love your enemies and pray for those who persecute you, so that you may be children of your Father in heaven; for he makes his sun rise on the evil and on the good, and sends rain on the righteous and on the unrighteous. For if you love those who love you, what reward do you have? Do not even the tax collectors do the same? And if you greet only your brothers and sisters, what more are you doing than others? Do not even the Gentiles do the same? Be perfect, therefore, as your heavenly Father is perfect.

The Sermon on the Mount teaches spiritual peace by teaching love. Through love comes individual spiritual maturity. The directive found in Matthew 5:44-8 confines this definition

---

[313] Michael Fagenblat, "The Concept of Neighbor in Jewish and Christian Ethics," in *The Jewish Annotated New Testament*, ed. Amy-Jill Levine and Marc Zvi Brettler (Oxford: Oxford University Press, 2011), 542.

[314] Stern, *Jewish New Testament Commentary*, 30.

[315] *Orchot Tzaddikim* is a book on Jewish ethics written in Germany in the 15th century, entitled *Sefer ha-Middot* by the author, but called *Orchot Tzaddikim* by a later copyist. Though this writing has no bearing on the Sermon on the Mount, Stern references the similarity of style and content of the two documents.

[316] Levine and Brettler, *The Jewish Annotated New Testament*, 12.

[317] Matthew 22:37-39 quotes the Jewish prayer the *Shema* taken from Deuteronomy 6:4-9.

of love to the audience to whom it was directed: Jewish-Christians. This text varies slightly from the Lukan version (6:27) in regards to identifying a sinner: Matthew equates sinners with tax collectors, while Luke just calls them sinners. In the Matthew version, one is to pray for those who persecute you. In the Lukan version (6:27), the word 'love' is replaced by the word 'good'. Vermes contends that the model of love is not limited exclusively to the Jewish people: "The model is universal. The term enemy, unless otherwise defined, normally suggests an outsider to the community of Israel... generally speaking Jesus' vision does not stretch beyond the Jewish world."[318]

The Sermon on the Mount requires maturity of its listeners. Levine and Brettler write, "Be perfect, (*teleios*). The word in this sense appears in the New Testament only in Matthew's Gospel and the Letter of James. It implies maturity or wisdom."[319] An example Jesus used, although not in the Sermon on the Mount, was the story of Zaccheus. The tax-collector in the Matthew account of the Sermon is a person who is or identifies as a sinful person and this person is not perfect (*teleios*). In the Matthew story, Zaccheus the tax collector "is a person rejected and despised."[320] According to Stern, a tax collector was a despised person in the Jewish community because they worked for the oppressive state and also lined their own pockets with money.[321] Tax collecting was given to those who offered the best bid for it, which meant the collection was open to abuse. The concept of 'loving your enemy' is important to understand from a historical perspective, as its understanding is dictated by contextual, ethical and political ideologies. The Jewish audience of the Sermon on the Mount

---

[318] Vermes, *The Religion of Jesus the Jew,* 157.

[319] Levine and Brettler, *The Jewish Annotated New Testament,* 12.

[320] Lachs, *A Rabbinic Commentary on the New Testament,* 109.

[321] Stern, *Jewish New Testament Commentary,* 30.

would have perceived that 'loving your enemy' is about 'doing good for them' in accordance with the dictates of their own era and culture.

3.3 **Conclusion**

The Sermon on the Mount birthed many of the peace ethics in the Christian Church, and may have been received initially by its Jewish listeners as a call to non-violence in the context of resistance. This way of resistance aligns itself with the *Mishna* and with the obligation to preserve one's Jewish identity. One of the most widely interpreted passages of scripture is the Sermon on the Mount and specifically the Beatitudes. The Sermon on the Mount was delivered primarily if not entirely to Jews, although debate remains as to which Jews these were. Some scholars claim that the Sermon was intended for the disciples, while others hold to the idea that the discourse was for all present—a multitude. The only certain fact we have is that in Matthew a group of people in political distress due to an oppressive foreign government receive a sermon. The content of the discourse was not intended to re-construct the judicial system of the day but rather to instruct people. In the Sermon on the Mount, no evidence points to a Gentile target audience. The Sermon in the Gospel of Matthew is divided into six segments, including the fulfilment of the law, murder, adultery, divorce, oaths, retributive justice and loving enemies. These represent an intensification of the law as opposed to an abrogation. Jesus also emphasises social ethics. A Gentile may not have so quickly embraced these ideas. The Sermon delves into meekness and humility, peacemaking and messianic ideals. Moving along logically, however, Jesus begins to balance the passivity of previous themes with a tone of non-violent 'resistance' through the discussion of turning the other cheek. The Jewish *mishna* similarly shows that this is not retaliation, rebellion or armed revolt but simply a preservation of human dignity. Jesus hints at issues of equality through a framework of peaceful yet creative justice. Turning a cheek, rendering one's underclothes to a lender in order to expose their greed under Mosaic law, and being unpredictable by carrying a soldier's load further than requested all point to an innovative and strategic form of non-violence. Here is a demand for an equality of sorts, and a learning to love one's enemies. Having covered the actual content of the Sermon, the next chapter will build on what has been examined thus far (the ethical understanding of the audience and the content of the sermon itself) in order to discover the implications of those same peace sayings for the Jewish listeners of the age.

CHAPTER 4

POLITICAL IMPLICATIONS OF THE PEACE SAYINGS

4.1 Introduction

The political implications of the peace sayings found in the Sermon on the Mount will now be viewed through the lens of Jewish ethical thought at the time of Jesus in order to understand the likely meaning for the Jewish listeners of the Sermon. Using Jewish ethical thought (as developed in Chapter Two) as the framework to interpret the peace sayings found within the Sermon on the Mount (as developed in Chapter Three) provides a likely understanding of those peace sayings for Jewish listeners. In order to develop a Jewish understanding of Jesus' Sermon on the Mount, one must accept that his audience, for the most part, saw Jesus as a rabbi or at least as a teacher. He would have been a Torah-observant man who provided an understanding of Jewish ethics. The Jewish listener would have understood the *Mishna* (at this time the oral sayings as discussed in Chapter Two) and processed Jesus' teaching from the Sermon on the Mount in light of them. Jesus' Torah observance is related to his observance of the *Mishna Avot*. "Reflecting on *Mishna Avot* and its commentaries provides an opportunity to begin formulating a Christian theology of the Torah," writes Joslyn-Siemiatkoski, "Such a theology must begin with premises about the degree of Torah observance by Jesus of Nazareth and the earliest followers of Jesus."[322]

When we apply the peace sayings of Jesus within a Jewish understanding of ethics in the *Mishna*, a Christian theology of the Torah emerges, combining understanding of the Sermon on the Mount with the *Mishna Avot*. The peaceful sayings of Jesus impact on how the Jewish people should respond to the Roman occupation. This chapter develops the concept that a

---

[322] Daniel Joslyn-Siemiatkoski, "Moses Received the Torah at Sinai and Handed It On Mishnah Avot 1:1," *Anglican Theological Review* 91, no. 3 (2009), 443.

Jewish leader was addressing a Jewish audience who were looking for a *moshiach* whom they could spiritually and politically follow; therefore, Jesus provides a political response of nonviolence. This political response for the Jewish listeners is demonstrated in Matthew 5:38-42 with the *turn the other cheek* phrase; however, it was not a call for social subjugation but for political and social equality for the person being slapped who was entitled to equal treatment. This rejects the degree to which Torah created legal equality under the Mosaic law for all followers of Torah. Jesus further explains this through *loving your enemy*, which provides a unique twist and a subsequent theology of love. Jesus' solidarity with Mosaic law showed continuity with the Jewish traditions which come from Hebrew Bible and the Jewish apocryphal writings.

4.2 Nonviolence as a Political Response

A nonviolent response to political oppression is the most likely Jewish way of interpreting Matthew 5:38-42 from the Sermon on the Mount. According to the *Mishna Avot*, the Jewish community who were familiar with the oral law avoided using unnecessary violence to resist violence. This is evident from the small number of civil uprisings before the destruction of the Temple and the way the Romans suppressed Jewish rebellions. In Chapter Two, Jewish ethical and political responses to violence were outlined, and the correlation between *Mishna Avot* 1:10, which advocates non-confrontational solutions to violence, and *Mishna Avot* 1:12, which advocates loving peace, were highlighted.[323] These teachings were contemporary with Jesus. These oral law sayings can be detected in the peace sayings in the Sermon on the Mount, specifically in the character of an individual as defined by Matthew 5:9 and the political response to violence defined in Matthew 5:39.

Perceptions about the characteristics of a community of people would have diverged between Roman and Jewish listeners. However, the writer of Matthew focuses on the Jewish

---

[323] The Roman-Jewish War of 66-73 CE and the Bar Kochba Rebellion demonstrate the rising tension for the Jews under Roman occupation.

perspective on the community and the impact on peaceful living of the interpretation of community building and self-preservation. The hierarchy of community leadership was appointed by the Romans from Jewish families, such as the Sadducees.[324] An attack on the Jewish community leadership is recorded by the author of Matthew in chapter 23: a sixfold "woe to you, Pharisees, scribes, and hypocrites."[325] This community of political leaders was to lead all Jews and Gentiles into a Jewish lifestyle and Torah observance.[326, 327] The author of Matthew attacks this community of leaders for shifting from the fundamental Jewish lifestyle of following the *mitzvoth* as well as law, economy, and customs of Jewish *halakha*. Some scholars think that this might have caused a rift in the Matthean community.[328] The Jewish people here are the Jewish-Christian minority who are struggling to follow all of the Torah and integrate into Roman society, which is causing Rome to scrutinize the Jewish-Christian minority.

Roman belief amalgamated the imperial mission into the culture; non-violent resistance against this imperial mission shows the Pharisees as protecting self-identity. The Jewish Pharisee mission and culture was to be a nonviolent response to the Roman mission to expand the political kingdom of the Empire. Carter writes regarding the Jewish-Christian community:

> This community also rejects violence, a mainstay of Rome's imperial mission to 'rule
>
> the nations with your power' (Virgil, *Aen.* 6.851-53). The cycle of violence is broken

---

[324] Saldarini, *Matthew's Christian-Jewish Community*, 48.

[325] Ibid., 52.

[326] Ibid., 49.

[327] The Talmud relates that some time before the destruction of the Second Temple in 70 CE, Rabbi Yohanan ben Zakkai relocated to the city of Yavne/Jamnia, where he received permission from the Romans to found a school of Halakha (Jewish law). Yavne was also the town where the Sanhedrin relocated after the destruction of the Temple. Zakkai's school became a major source for the later *Mishna*, which records the work of the Tannaim, and a wellspring of Rabbinic Judaism.

[328] Saldarini, *Matthew's Christian-Jewish Community*, 49.

not by matching violence with violence, nor by passivity, but by a third option.

Instead of fight or flight, Matthew's Jesus advocates nonviolent resistance to evil

(5:38-42).[329]

The message of Jesus builds upon the existing Jewish sayings and applies those ethical

and moral sayings to the context relevant to those who were listening to the Sermon. This

building upon prior sages does not negate the importance of Jesus but demonstrates how

Jesus' sayings were acceptable to those listening to the Sermon because they were a part of

the culture's oral law. The message of a third way, which is non-violent resistance, builds

upon the verb (*antistenai*) in 5:39, "which does not mean 'do not resist an evildoer,' an

impossible though regrettably common translation. Rather it denotes (with a negative) not

using violence to resist evil."[330] A plausible understanding would be to not use violence to

resist an evildoer in Matthew 5: 38-42 in relation to slapping. Jesus sets out in Matthew 5:38-

42 four examples of what such resistance might look like in actions that refuse submission,

assert human dignity, and challenge what is supposed to humiliate and destroy.[331] These

examples build upon existing Jewish intellectual thought common to all Jewish men who

studied Torah before their *bar mitzvah,* and they build Jesus' unique understanding as a

teacher of Torah. The thought of Jesus liberates people, gives them dignity and challenges

that which is destroying them.

The writer of Matthew calls on the political leadership of the community to adhere to

Jewish standards as advocated by Jesus through love.[332] The word 'nation' in the only use of

this term in Matthew 24:7 is a translation of the Greek word *ethnos* which means 'band,

---

[329] Carter, *Matthew and Empire*, 127.

[330] Ibid.

[331] Ibid.

[332] Saldarini, *Matthew's Christian-Jewish Community,* 52.

people, class, or nation'.[333] Thus, the leadership and the people are called to a greater Torah observant lifestyle by going beyond the normal life.

In Matthew 5:39, the Jewish audience's understanding of non-retaliation would lead them to directly oppose the Zealots who sought to militarily overthrow Roman rule. Non-retaliation was a part of Jewish culture.[334] Talbert points out that non-retaliation was a part of the Jewish tradition, stating that "Jewish evidence includes; 1QS 10.17-20; *Joseph and Aseneth* 23:9—'it does not befit us to repay evil for evil;' *b. Shabbat* 88b; *2 Enoch* 50:3-4."[335] [336] This concept of non-retaliation was far from being 'new' to both Jews and selected Gentiles, even if it was not mainstream.

Matthew 5:38-42 portrays the Jesus movement as peace activism for self-preservation. The Sermon on the Mount's Jewish listeners, possibly simple non-intellectuals (who understood *Pirkei Avot* 1:10 "to love your brother" in conjunction with the directive "to have justice" in the *Avot* 2:7) balanced nonviolence and peace with the need for personal survival under oppressive rulers. Those who became Jewish-Christians followed non-violent resistance. Borg writes, "As the peace party in Palestine, the Jesus movement thus rejected the path of violent resistance to Rome. The people of God were not to secure their existence through the force of arms or violence; faithfulness pointed to another way."[337] The *Mishna* taught compassion in charity and non-confrontation in *Avot* 1:10, which is synonymous with the nonviolent teachings of the Sermon on the Mount in which, "[t]he spirit of resistance was

---

[333] Ibid, 59.

[334] Talbert, *Reading the Sermon on the Mount*, 89.

[335] Ibid.

[336] Other Jewish texts that encourage non-retaliation are Exodus 23:4-5; Leviticus 19:18; Proverbs 20:22, 24:29.

[337] Marcus J. Borg, *Jesus: A New Vision* (London: SPCK, 1994), 139.

countered."[338] The perceived need for resistance was not to excuse or validate the use of violence; trust in God would secure safety without arms in the Jewish context unless the survival of the people was in question.

4.3 Slapping and Social Equality

The Jewish understanding of slapping and social equality shapes a peaceful interpretation of the Sermon on the Mount. As seen in Chapter Two, the *lex talionis* defines the response a Jewish believer would give toward another person with whom a disagreement occurred. Social equality played an important role in interpreting the peace sayings because the poor were at risk of being taken advantage of by the rich classes. Slapping is a form of retaliation regulated by *Pirkei Avot* 2:15, *Pirkei Avot* 1:12, *Pirkei Avot* 1:10, *Pirkei Avot* 2:17, and *Pirkei Avot* 3:16. The Jewish listener who had studied or heard the saying may have avoided conflict. In Chapter Three, the definition of resistance was explored in the context of Matthew 5:39.

The scenario depicted in Matthew 5:39 suggests turning the other cheek as a response to being slapped by another person. There are two ways a person can slap another person— either with the front of the hand or the back of the hand. The slap may be an open-handed slap as in Matthew 5:39, 26:27, Hosea 11:4, and 1 Esdras 4:30.[339] If this type of slap was involved then both participants would be social equals; however, in the Sermon on the Mount this is not specified. One could assume that the situation was not between social peers, because one could not be socially equal and hit someone on the right cheek unless left-handed. A left-handed slap still makes slapping a newly presented cheek on the other side quite difficult (but slapping with the left hand was simply not done due to it being the hand used for toilet needs). Moreover, there is vagueness in the Matthew text regarding the

---

[338] Ibid., 137-38.

[339] Davis, *Lex Talionis in Early Judaism and the Exhortation of Jesus in Matthew 5:38-42*, 142.

ethnicity of those who are slapping and being slapped. "Jesus is saying, if you are slapped on the cheek of inferiority [as in being backhanded], turn to the offender the cheek of equal dignity."[340] A backhanded slap was associated with the demeaning slap for those of lower status, such as slaves and women.

The best approach way to understand the slap is as a backhanded one because the openhanded slap was not done between people who were socially unequal. When a person is backhanded, "one's first response to such an insult might be physical retaliation, a backhanded slap in kind."[341] The insulting backhanded slap on the left cheek, when juxtaposed with turning the right cheek, is a demand for equality because one person is placed in power over another person.[342] Turning the "other" cheek implies that it "was the most offensive, insulting and humiliating kind of slap."[343] Once the cheek was turned, however, the newly presented cheek would be hard to backhand. To hit the cheek that was presented would require a punch. A punch to the face or other such hit would be reserved for a peer—and would often come with a fine under Roman law.

The ethical and political implication of turning the other cheek is personified in the trial of Jesus. When Jesus was slapped, "Jesus himself did not turn the other cheek when struck at his trial, but rather challenged the smiter, 'why do you strike me?' (Jn. 18:23)."[344] The text states "Jesus answered, "If I have spoken wrongly, testify to the wrong. But if I have spoken rightly, why do you strike me?" Although initially seeming to contradict the Sermon on the Mount, it illustrates the way a person who is slapped should act when powerless. Thus, Jesus' words actually support the nonviolent lesson of the Sermon on the Mount. Lachs suggests that if

---

[340] Stassen and Gushee, *Kingdom Ethics*, 139.

[341] Davis, *Lex Talionis in Early Judaism*, 142.

[342] Ibid.

[343] Ibid.

[344] William Swartley, *Slavery, Sabbath, War & Women* (Scottsdale, AZ: Herald, 1983), 101.

you are struck by someone in authority over you, "you must forgive the offender even though he does not ask for your forgiveness" as a form of nonviolent action.[345] Jesus personifies non-violent action, in contrast to Peter the disciple in the Garden of Gethsemane, who cut off the ear of the High Priest's servant (John 18:10). Richard Burridge supports the theory that slapping on the cheek, as described in the Sermon on the Mount, refers to a dehumanising action, while turning the cheek and making further slaps difficult is a way of asserting one's humanity and social equality. He says, "While Luke suggests simply being hit in the face Matthew's specifying 'the right cheek' (Matt. 5:39; cp. Luke 6:29) entails a more insulting back-handed blow dealt by a superior like a master to a slave or 'the religious elite with dangerous preacher'."[346] While often considered another invitation to abuse, turning the cheek is actually a demand for equality and constitutes a non-violent protest.

There is a second type of response to a slap on the left cheek that is legal retaliation through the court system.[347] By not retaliating, by not slapping an aggressor in return, the victim forces the oppressor to use other legal means to seek justice. The justice afforded protects a person from wrongdoing by a person in power. If a person who was slapped by another person decided to take the transgressor to court, then they were supporting justice through the state's legal system.

4.4 Legal Equality under Mosaic Law

Relevant to the peace sayings for the Jewish listeners of the Sermon on the Mount were Jewish legal customs regarding conflicts. While living under Roman occupation, the Jewish people were under Roman law; however, they were allowed to have a Mosaic court to

---

[345] Lachs, *A Rabbinic Commentary on the New Testament*, 104.

[346] Richard A. Burridge, *Imitating Jesus* (Grand Rapids, MI: Eerdmans, 2007), 216.

[347] Davis, *Lex Talionis in Early Judaism*, 142.

regulate Jewish religious matters. In the Sermon on the Mount, the application of the Mosaic law is explained in Matthew 5:40 which states "and if someone wants to sue you and take your tunic, let him have your cloak as well." The behaviour defined through charity is tantamount to Jewish ethical behaviour; similarly, the implication of a Jewish individual seeking a peaceful yet charitable legal remedy is a part of Jewish identity. The ethical implication of seeking justice and equality in the legal system between two opposing litigating parties, "because the [Jewish] law did not permit taking away a man's cloak overnight, for fear he might freeze to death while sleeping [Exodus 22.26-27; Deut. 24. 12-13].[348] The legal protection afforded to those who borrowed money was discussed in Chapter Two.[349] This foundation for money lending extends to the collection of that money.

The Roman state taxed the citizenry and the subjects of Rome and the individual worked desperately to find ways to pay these taxes. Allison indicates that Matthew 5:40 extends beyond the legal court system to ethical actions committed in private lives: "It is true that 5:40 refers to the court; but Jesus is not here delivering laws for the court to follow (cf. Hagner, Matthew 1-13, ad loc.). Jesus provides further understanding of *lex talionis* by suggesting it is illegitimate for his followers to apply the *lex talionis* to their private problems."[350] By empowering the individual to act ethically, justice is served. Burridge explains how the listeners to the Sermon on the Mount would seek justice:

> Jesus tells his hearers to hand over their [cloak] also. While this has traditionally been seen as a call to being meek and submissive, interpreters like Wink and Carter see it more as nonviolent resistance to evil: By standing naked before one's creditor who has both garments in his hand, one shames and dishonors the creditor. Nakedness

---

[348] Burridge, *Imitating Jesus, 216.*

[349] Religious law protected citizens in *Pirkei Avot* 2:14, Psalms 37:21 and Proverbs 22:7.

[350] Dale C. Allison, *The Sermon on the Mount* (New York: Crossroad, 1999), 93.

exposes, among other things, the greed and cruel effect of the creditor's action and the unjust system the creditor represents.[351]

The social pressure to be non-violent, highlighted by Wink and Carter in Chapter Two, created ethical judicial systems and provided justice for those who were Jewish. Not acting aggressively against a collector of debt is balanced with *Pirkei Avot,* which suggests that the path against the evil person is to ignore his debts. The nonviolent approach presented to those who listened to the Sermon on the Mount was one of resisting evil. *Avot* 2:14 states,

> He said to them: Go out and see which is the evil path which a man should avoid. Rabbi Eliezer said, an evil eye. Rabbi Joshua said, an evil companion. Rabbi Yosi said, an evil neighbor. Rabbi Shimon said, One who borrows and does not repay. One who borrows from another is like one who borrows from God, for it is written (Psalm 37:21) 'The wicked borrows and does not pay back, but the righteous is generous and gives.' Rabbi Elazar said, an evil heart. He said to them: I prefer the words of Elazar ben Arakh more than your words, for in his words your words are included.[352]

Legal equality between the political oppressor and the oppressed better ensures a fair and ethical treatment of people. The listener to the Sermon on the Mount knew that a person who failed to repay debts was evil; similarly, he would have understood that "giving your cloak as well" would expose those who were lending without ethical means.

4.5 Loving your Enemy and its Political Implications

The call of Matthew 5:39 to "love your enemy" inspires non-violence against political aggression. Loving your enemies is more than non-retaliation; the call in Matthew 5:39 is a "specific political response to centuries of violence and to the contemporary Zealots' call for

---

[351] Ibid.

[352] Psalm 37:21 (JPS).

violent revolution" through the act of positively loving others.[353] Love brings a safer way and new insights into victory over enemies through a peaceful non-violent paradigm of love.

The teachings of Jesus that command love for an enemy refer to Jews and Gentiles alike when they are enslaved and when they are in power. There is an ethical obligation to love all people across both Jews and non-Jews:

> In the same context where Jesus spoke of the *Imitatio Dei* as compassion, he also spoke of loving one's enemies: 'You have heard that it was said, 'Love your neighbor,' but I say to you, Love your enemies.' The quoted words, 'Love your neighbor,' come from the holiness code and were understood within contemporary Judaism to mean, 'Love your fellow member of the covenant,' that is, your fellow Israelite or compatriot. In this context, the opposite of neighbor is clearly 'non-Israelite,' and so loving one's enemy must mean, 'Love the non-Israelite enemy,' including the Gentile occupiers.[354]

The Jewish listener to the Sermon on the Mount would have understood the ethical implications of Jesus' teaching because the sayings found in *Pirkei Avot* were common knowledge during the time of Jesus and offer an alternative way of non-violent resistance and love for the Gentile. *Avot* 2:17 qualifies one's deeds, "Let all your deeds be done for the sake of Heaven," and *Avot* 3:16 elaborates, "Rabbi Ishmael says: Be submissive to the ruler and patient with oppression. Receive everyone with cheerfulness." This paradigm of loving your enemy generates a political implication of collegiality amongst those who don't get along which ultimately fosters non-violence.

4.6 Jesus Demonstrates Solidarity with Mosaic Laws

---

[353] Swartley, *Slavery, Sabbath, War & Women*, 121.

[354] Borg, *Jesus: A New Vision*, 137.

The ways people respond to each other and to the state provide the political implications of the Sermon on the Mount. They are apparent in the correlation that Jesus maintains between the Mosaic laws and the peace sayings. The Mosaic laws are upheld by Jesus in the gospel of Matthew, who provides an example to his listeners of how to follow the Roman laws and still maintain Jewish observance by advocating peaceful action. Jews who keep the *mitzvoth* also had a connection with Mosaic law. The understanding of what constitutes being peaceful depended upon the level of *mitzvoth* observance of the Jewish person listening to the Sermon: Sabbath keeping, commerce, and festival observance were important to some of the listeners and determined whether they would follow the laws.[355] The level of Jesus' Torah observance is a contentious topic; however, Jesus seems to have followed Torah described in the gospel of Matthew. Although Jesus was concerned with gentiles so some degree, Jesus' own perspective was exclusively Jewish; he was concerned only with Jews.[356] He observed the Sabbath in Matthew 12:1, he used money in the Temple in Matthew 21:12, and he observed the Passover in Matthew 26:2; all of these examples illustrate how Jesus followed *mitzvoth*. As Jonathan G. Campbell points out, "the scriptures making up the canonical Torah were fixed in early post-exilic times," and all Israelites of the Second Temple period would have studied and interpreted the same Torah, encountering the same laws therein.[357] Even the early Jewish-Christians considered themselves Jews in their outward behaviour and dietary customs by observing all of the Mosaic law.[358]

In Matthew 5:40, Jesus draws upon the text of Exodus 22:26. Saldarini writes: "In first-century Judaism, interpretation of the law was a political act in which the control of society

---

[355] Ibid., 127-8.

[356] Geza Vermes, "From Jewish to Gentile," *Biblical Archaeology Review,* volume 38, number 6 (2012), 53.

[357] Jonathan G. Campbell, "4QMMT and the Tripartite Canon," *Journal of Jewish Studies,* volume 51, number 2 (2000), 184.

[358] Vermes, "From Jewish to Gentile," 54.

was at stake. Disagreements among groups involved substantial conflict over public laws and norms."[359] The sayings of Jesus embrace the rule of law and create a political climate that provides stability between the Mosaic law and the political system by having the Jesus movement work with the political state instead of revolting against it. Jesus' statements call upon Mosaic teaching:

> This is the minimum assertion that can be made. The consistency can be even greater emphasized if we ground our remarks in the authority of the courts under the Old Testament and the moral obligation to obey them. Jesus' embracing the rule of law— of the right of courts to make decisions (even mistaken ones) concerning use— embraces (rather than rejects) the teaching of the Mosaic system.[360]

The sayings of Jesus found in the Sermon on the Mount are similar to the discussion found in Chapter Two providing an ethical understanding of Jewish thought. The Jewish listener would have understood that the Jewish Jesus was perpetuating and expounding existing Jewish law.[361] Such an audience would have embraced the peace sayings as an inherent part of traditional Jewish teachings: "Here Jesus' teaching in substance is not radically divergent from that recorded in *Mishna Avot.* Just as the rabbis in *Avot* emphasize the importance of keeping the Torah, so Jesus embraces the Torah."[362] While often thought of as teaching 'new' concepts, Jesus reiterated the old, the traditional and the known, according to the author of Matthew.[363] Jesus' observance of halakhic issues are at the heart of Jewish sectarianism.[364]

---

[359] Saldarini, *Matthew's Christian-Jewish Community*, 124.

[360] Worth, *The Sermon on the Mount*, 224.

[361] Saldarini, *Matthew's Christian-Jewish Community*, 125.

[362] John Oslyn-Siemiatkoski, "Moses Received the Torah at Sinai and Handed It On. Mishnah Avot 1:1: The Relevance of the Written and Oral Torah for Christians," *Anglican Theological Review* 91, no. 3 (2009), 463.

[363] Saldarini, *Matthew's Christian-Jewish Community*, 126.

Jesus typified an observant Jew by upholding the Law while the Pharisees wonder if Jesus did not observe halakhic law. His solidarity with Mosaic law did not negate the Mosaic law but provided a midrash on aspects that were pertinent to the needs of those living in his time. The peace sayings did not create new doctrine or theology but allowed Jesus to apply the already known oral law to the contemporary Jew because Jesus spoke with authority as a rabbi of the law (Matthew 7:29). This fresh approach was unique to Jesus and valuable to the listeners.

4.7 Dead Sea Scrolls and Political Implications

The Dead Sea Scrolls help to provide an understanding of the political climate evolving during the time of Jesus. As seen in Chapter Three, the Dead Sea Scrolls provide insight into the mindset of some possible listeners to the Sermon on the Mount. Some Jews during the time of Jesus may have come into contact with the Essene community, whose influence quite possibly extended throughout the land. The Essene community both limited violence and produced a pseudo-war scroll.[365] The *War Scroll* has a similarity with other scrolls (4Q491-497; 4Q471; 4Q285, 11Q14) found in the Qumran caves which discuss the acceptance of religiously premeditated violence.[366] These scrolls advocate a religiously founded discussion of political violence.[367] Roman war manuals would have been precise and militaristic at least in form and style when advocating maneuvers on the battlefield; however, the *War Scroll* was not written to fight a military war. It foresees a forty-year eschatological war between two forces: the Children of Light, who will fight with the support of God and his angels, and the Children of Darkness who are allied with a demonic force lead by an evil spirit named Belial.

---

[364] Ibid., 5.

[365] Jassen,"The Dead Sea Scrolls and Violence," 13.

[366] Steven Weitzman.,"Warring against Terror: The War Scroll and the Mobilization of Emotion," *Journal for the Study of Judaism* 40, no. 2 (2009), 215.

[367] Ibid., 216.

The *War Scroll* was not a guide for real-life violence. In the plans drawn for those who would come to battle with evil, the Children of Light would follow a precisely scripted plan, frequently pausing to perform rituals and utter hymns. Some scholars have gone so far as to propose that the *War Scroll* is a script for some kind of liturgical drama or ritual rehearsal for the End of Days enacted by the members of the Qumran sect, rather than an actual battle.[368]

Josephus identifies an individual named Judah, the Essene, as a participant in the revolt against Rome (*War* 2:567) and, similarly, Philo notes that the Essenes were opposed to warfare (*Prob.* 78). Josephus elsewhere remarks that the Essenes refrained from all robbery, and he used the vocabulary regularly that others used for revolutionaries.[369] [370] The violence and the apocalyptic ideologies that seem so widespread among Jews (and the Jewish Christians) were introduced into the writings describing the Essenes and their legitimate role.[371]

The importance of the Dead Sea Scrolls is that they remind us that Jews at the time of Jesus expected a messianic figure with biblical ethical views.[372] The listener would expect some Jewish believers - if not the group – to avoid war.[373] The Dead Sea Scrolls record different views by Jews at the time of Jesus, and this sheds light on the political implications of those who may have been in contention against Roman rule from 66 CE to 73 CE, although some were nonviolent. As well, the Dead Sea Scrolls demonstrate that some from

---

[368] Ibid., 218.

[369] Jassen, "The Dead Sea Scrolls and Violence," 13.

[370] The political implications for the Essene community and non-violence rest in the replacement of the Hasmonean priestly line with the Zadokite line in the *escheton*, which will restore and purify the Temple.

[371] Hanan, *The Dead Sea Scrolls and the Hasmonean State*, 181.

[372] Saldarini, *Matthew's Christian-Jewish Community*, 126-7.

[373] Ibid.

the Qumran community practiced *tzedakah*, justice and truth, as seen in 1QS 1:5 and this practice impacted on how people lived a just life in society.[374]

4.8 Conclusion

The political implication of the peace sayings found in the Sermon is non-violence as a political response to oppression. By showing how the role of the Roman Empire conflicted with the peace sayings found in *Mishna Avot,* Jews who applied oral law in their life were being shown how to live a non-violent life. This chapter explored the message of non-violent resistance and the chapter builds upon the Greek verb (*antistenai*) to demonstrate how the political implications of peace offer a non-violent solution to violence by Roman rule.

While living under Roman occupation, the Jewish people were under Roman law; however, they were allowed to have a Mosaic court to regulate Jewish religious matters. In the Mosaic court, the Jewish people could seek economic redress for violations of Mosaic law. Violations of Roman law were dealt accordingly by the Roman court. The political implications of creating a non-violent response to political oppression were the development and improvement of the legal system. The message of legal equality under the Mosaic law was re-affirmed by Jesus' peace sayings, which build upon the existing Jewish sayings and apply those ethical and moral sayings to the context relevant to those listening to the Sermon. This building upon prior sages demonstrates how Jesus' sayings were acceptable to those listening to the Sermon because they affirmed a part of the culture's oral law on legal equality.

The way that Jesus offers non-violent resistance in Matthew 5:38-42 creates political implications for Rome. The unique midrash that Jesus provides in the Sermon on peace provides a stark contrast for all people living under the Roman imperial mission who were

---

[374] Saldarini, *Matthew's Christian-Jewish Community,* 142.

being oppressed and forced to carry military packs. The call to receive everyone with cheerfulness is a paradigm of loving your enemy with a non-violent political implication. The collegiality amongst those who don't get along ultimately fosters non-violence.

CHAPTER 5

CONCLUSION

The purpose of this dissertation has been to investigate the peace sayings found in the Sermon on the Mount and the likely understanding of them by those who heard them first. This dissertation found:

1. That the Jewish intellectual framework within which Jesus' first audience heard the Sermon on the Mount contains many specific sayings found in *Pirkei Avot* and also much non-violent action found in Jewish tradition; and

2. That the oral law and the Sermon on the Mount both reflect Jewish ethical ideologies of non-violent resistance.

Chapter Two investigated how non-violence originates from the biblical sources, which define a 'kingdom of peace' and the person of the *moshiach*. Chapter Two demonstrated how the *Mishna* came about, correlating it with the Jewish thought until the life of Jesus. Jewish thought in relation to a forthcoming *moshiach* both enhanced and hindered how non-violent actions would bring about the echaton for the non-Torah observant person. Further understanding of nonviolence rests in such Jewish writings as *Pirkei Avot*, which create the standards of behaviour for a community of people through the ethical sayings of the Jewish fathers during the time of Jesus.

The teachings of the Sermon on the Mount empowered people with a sense of dignity, promoting not a self-destructive violence against the oppressing powers but a sense of dignity and equality—a liberation of sorts in the face of tyranny. To a people with knowledge of *lex talionis* in the Jewish way of life, the Sermon on the Mount did not radically change or redefine known approaches to nonviolent actions but created a harmony between Jews who were listening and expecting a political change from Roman rule. Chapter Two also showed how Jesus provided a novel understanding of Jewish thought by showing how non-violence applied to their current life. *Tzedakah* created an ethical paradigm for interacting with each other through the regulation of loans. As well, *tzedakah* allowed charity for the Jewish person as a means of survival; thus, human dignity is vital to Jewish ethical thought as explained in the *Mishna* as well as in Matthew.

In Chapter Three, the Sermon on the Mount in Matthew 5:38-42 and its peace sayings were examined. Chapter Three described the audience of the Sermon as a predominately Jewish audience and the gospel of Matthew as a composition reflecting Jewish authorship. The Sermon is divided into six antitheses; however, the peace sayings are found through the Sermon. Jesus advocated non-violence as a political response to the Roman Empire and not a call for individual self-sacrifice. He never promoted the Zealots' mission of revolt, but he also never encouraged peacemaking to the point of renouncing human dignity. Chapter Three defines the peace sayings of the Sermon on the Mount as Matthew 5:5, 9 (meekness), 39 (peacemakers), 40 (equality), 41 (oppression from the state), and 43-48 (loving enemies).

Meekness was defined in Chapter Three as a characteristic of a humble person who attempts to create peace. Peacemakers are defined in Matthew 5:9 as people who are happy by walking righteously with God creating peace in the world. Matthew 5:39 defines resistance as increasing violence through retaliation. By turning the other cheek, the audience would have understood it not as an invitation for further abuse but as a creative demand for social equality. The instruction to expose an oppressor in court by handing over one's underwear is a method that brings shame and disgrace upon the accuser, while relieving the sense of helpless victimhood in the accused. Shame as a tool to promote individual justice and equality demonstrates how Jews listening to Jesus would understand that humans are equal and should abide by moral codes and law found in the Torah.

Chapter Three discussed Job 16:10, Lamentations 3:28-30 and Isaiah 50:6 which define the doctrine of restraint and equality through the judicial system. Jesus did not preach retaliation, which would ultimately have been fatal to Jewish listeners, but sought a safer way of loving enemies through a non-violent paradigm of love, respect, and doing good *mitzvoth* for others. Turning the other cheek when slapped was treated in *Pirkei Avot*. Escalating negative violence contradicts the Jewish oral law. While this may have introduced a new *emphasis* to the listeners (as the ethics of loving one's *neighbour* was commonly accepted), it was nonetheless in accordance with Mosaic Scriptures and a reiteration in accord with traditional and undisputed Jewish law.

Chapter Four combines the development of the peace sayings found in the Sermon (as examined in Chapter Three) with Jewish intellectual thought and ethics (as developed in Chapter Two). The result is to make clear that the audience of the Sermon would have heard Jesus promoting an alternative way of non-violent resistance to the political state. Jesus' sayings are unique because Jesus applied them to the current political situation. His listeners heard him take both pre and post Hasmonean biblical texts and apply them to the relationship between the Roman Empire and the Jewish people. There is no doubt that Jewish ethical and political thought up to and during the life of Jesus would have impacted on the ancient reception of Jesus' Sermon on the Mount by defining equality, slapping, loving, and the role of the Mosaic law. While the Bible teaches a kingdom of peace, a messianic leader and a people of peace, the oral law also contributes to the basic understanding of ancient Jewish justice and ethics. With a variety of ethical codes in the *Pirkei Avot*, Dead Sea Scrolls and the pseudepigrapha, the *lex talionis* and other non-direct sources such as the Code of Hammurabi, the ethical and political understanding of the audience of the Sermon on the Mount pivots on its view of justice, self-defence, retaliatory action, charity, and fiscal ethics. The Sermon itself, a Jewish discourse by a Jew to mainly Jews, centres upon meekness, peacemaking, resisting, equality, oppression by the state and loving one's enemies. These concepts would have been comprehended through a Jewish framework of understanding by the listeners to the Sermon on the Mount. Chapter Four applies the cumulative discussion of *Mishna* to the peace saying of Jesus, and while we cannot claim to know for certain the thoughts of the audience, we can make an educated guess. In the cases of cheek slapping, cloak stripping, and mile walking, the emphasis is on a non-violent form of resistance that not only liberates the oppressed but also renders a sense of empowerment and human dignity to the abused.

BIBLIOGRAPHY

Allison, Dale C. *The Sermon on the Mount*. New York: Crossroad, 1999.

Bauckham, Richard. The Jewish World Around The New Testament. Grand Rapids, MI: Baker, 2008.

Berlin, Adele and Marc Zvi Brettler. "Deuteronomy." In *The Jewish Study Bible*, ed. Bernard M. Levinson, 356-450. Oxford: Oxford University Press, 2004.

Betz, Hans Dieter. *Essays on the Sermon on the Mount*. Philadelphia, PA: Fortress, 1985.

Blackman, Philip. *Tractate Avoth*. Gateshead, UK: Judaica, 1979.

_____. *Ethics of the Fathers*. Gateshead, UK: Judaica, 1979.

Borg, Marcus J. *Jesus: A New Vision*. London: SPCK, 1994.

Borkowski, Andrew. *Roman Law*. London: Blackstone, 1994.

Boyarin, Daniel. *The Jewish Gospels*. New York: The New Press, 2012.

Burridge, Richard A. *Imitating Jesus*. Grand Rapids, MI: Eerdmans, 2007.

Campbell, Jonathan G. "4QMMT and the Tripartite Canon." *Journal of Jewish Studies* volume 51, number 2, 2000: 181-190.

Carson, D. A. and Douglas J. Moo. *An Introduction to the New Testament*. Grand Rapids, MI: Zondervan, 2005.

Carter, Warren. "Evoking Isaiah: Matthean Soteriology and an Intertextual Reading of Isaiah 7-9 and Matthew 1:23 and 4:15-16." *Journal of Biblical Literature* 119, no. 3 (2000): 503-520.

_____. *Matthew and Empire*. Harrisburg, PA: Trinity, 2001.

Cohen, Beryl D. *Jacob's Well: Some Jewish Sources and Parallels to the Sermon on the Mount*. New York: Bookman, 1956.

Collins, John J. *Beyond the Qumran Community: The Sectarian Movement of the Dead Sea Scrolls*. Grand Rapids, MI: Eerdmans, 2011.

Crossley, James G. "Book Review of *Lex Talionis in Early Judaism and the Exhortation of Jesus in Matthew 5:38-42*." *Journal for the Study of the New Testament*, 58, no. 1 (2006): 200-201.

Davies, W. D., and Dale C. Allison. *Matthew 1-7*, International Critical Commentary. Edinburgh: T & T Clark, 1988.

Davis, James F. *Lex Talionis in Early Judaism and the Exhortation of Jesus in Matthew 5:38-42*. New York: T&T Clark, 2005.

Davis, W. W. *The Codes of Hammurabi and Moses*. New York: Cosimo, 2010.

DeSilva, David A. *The Jewish Teachers of Jesus, James, and Jude*. Oxford: Oxford University Press, 2012.

Eisenman, Robert H., and Michael Wise. *The Dead Sea Scrolls Uncovered*. New York: Barnes and Noble, 2004.

Enslin, Morton Scott. *Christian Beginnings* Part I. New York: Harper & Row, 1956.

Fagenblat, Michael. "The Concept of Neighbor in Jewish and Christian Ethics." In *The Jewish Annotated New Testament*, eds. Amy-Jill Levine and Marc Zvi Brettler, 540-543, Oxford: Oxford University Press, 2011.

Fahey, Joseph J. *War and the Christian Conscience*. Maryknoll, NY: Orbis, 2008.

Gamoran, Hillel. *Talmud For Everyday Living*. New York: UAHC, 2001.

Gibson, Edgar C.S. *Commentary on the Book of Job*, Westminster Commentary Series. Greenwood, SC: Attic, 1976.

Goulder, M. D. *Midrash and Lection in Matthew*. London: SPCK, 1977.

Habel, Norman C. *Jeremiah/ Lamentations*, Concordia Commentary. St. Louis, MO: Concordia, 1968.

Hagner, Donald A. *Matthew 1-13*, Word Biblical Commentary, vol. 33a. Nashville, TN: Thomas Nelson, 1993.

Hanan, Eshel. *The Dead Sea Scrolls and the Hasmonean State*. Grand Rapids: Eerdmans, 2008.

Hays, Richard B. *The Moral Vision of the New Testament*. San Francisco, CA: Harper Collins, 1996.

Hill, Craig C. *In God's Time: The Bible and the Future*. Grand Rapids, MI: Eerdmans, 2002.

Hirschfeld, Yizhar. *Qumran in Context: Reassessing the Archaeological Evidence*. Peabody, MA: Baker Academic, 2004.

Hodge, Stephen. *The Dead Sea Scrolls Rediscovered*. Berkeley, CA: Seastone, 2003.

Horsley, Richard A. *Scribes, Visionaries, and the Politics of Second Temple Judea*. London: Westminster John Knox, 2007.

Instone-Brewer, David. *Traditions of the Rabbis from the Era of the New Testament* 2a. Grand Rapids, MI: Eerdmans, 2011.

Jacobs, Jill. *There Shall Be No Needy*. Woodstock, VT: Jewish Lights, 2009.

Jassen, Alex. "The Dead Sea Scrolls and Violence: Sectarian Formation and Eschatological Imagination." *Biblical Interpretation* 17, nos. 1-2 (2009): 12-44.

Joslyn-Siemiatkoski, Daniel. "Moses Received the Torah at Sinai and Handed It On (Mishnah Avot 1:1)." *Anglican Theological Review* 91, no. 3 (2009): 433-466.

Keener, Craig S. *The Gospel of Matthew: A Socio-Rhetorical Commentary*. Grand Rapids, MI: Eerdmans, 2009.

Kennedy, George. *New Testament Interpretation Through Rhetorical Criticism*. Chapel Hill, NC: University of North Carolina Press, 1984.

Kravitz, Leonard and Kerry Olitzky. *Pirke Avot*. New York: UAHC, 1993.

Lachs, Samuel Tobias. *A Rabbinic Commentary on the New Testament*. Hoboken, NJ: KTAV, 1987.

Lapide, Pinchas. *The Sermon on the Mount*. New York: Orbis, 1986.

Lawler, Andrew. "Who Wrote the Dead Sea Scrolls?" *Smithsonian* 40, no. 10 (2010): 40.

Lee, Bernard J. *The Galilean Jewishness of Jesus*. New York: Paulist, 1988.

Levine, Amy-Jill. *The Misunderstood Jew*. New York: HarperOne, 2007.

Levine, Amy-Jill, and Marc Zvi Brettler. *The Jewish Annotated New Testament*. Oxford: Oxford University Press, 2011.

Levine, Amy-Jill, Dale C. Allison Jr, and John Dominic Crossan. *The Historical Jesus in Context*. Princeton, NJ: Princeton University Press, 2006.

Lieber, Moshe. *The Pirkei Avos Treasury*. vol. 1. Brooklyn, NY: Mesorah, 1997.

_____. *The Pirkei Avos Treasury*. vol. 2. Brooklyn, NY: Mesorah, 1996.

Mandel, Morris, and Samson Krupnick. *Torah Dynamics*. Spring Valley, NY: Feldheim, 1991.

McComiskey, Bruce. "Laws, Works, and the End of Days: Rhetorics of Identification, Distinction, and Persuasion in (Dead Sea Scroll 4QMMT)." *Rhetoric Review* 29, no. 3 (2010): 221-238.

Meier, John P. *A Marginal Jew*. vol. 4. London: Yale University Press, 2009.

Miller, Robert J. *The Complete Gospels*. Santa Rosa, CA: Polebridge, 1992.

Neusner, Jacob. *Making God's Word Work: a guide to the Mishnah*. New York: Continuum

International, 2004.

_____, and Bruce Chilton. *Judaism in the New Testament*. London: Routledge, 1995.

_____, William S Green, and Ernest Grerichs. *Judaisms and their Messiahs*. Cambridge: Cambridge University Press, 1990.

Nickelsburg, George W. E. "First and Second Enoch: A Cry against Oppression and the Promise of Deliverance." In *The Historical Jesus in Context*, eds. Amy-Jill Levine, Dale C. Allison Jr and John Dominic Crossan, 87-110. Princeton, NJ: Princeton University Press, 2006.

Novenson, Matthew V. "Why Does R. Akiba Acclaim Bar Kokhba as Messiah?" *Journal for the Study of Judaism* 40, nos. 4-5 (2009): 551-572.

Pazola, Ron. "Can the Dead Sea Scrolls teach us about the living Jesus?" *U.S. Catholic* 58, no.11 (1993): 13-20.

Reichart, Victor E. *Job: With Hebrew Text and English Translation*. Hindhead, Surrey, UK: Soncino, 1946.

Reichberg, Gregory M. "Thomas Aquinas Between Just War and Pacifism." *Journal of Religious Ethics* 38, no. 2, (2010): 219-241.

Reiss, Moshe. "Cyrus as Messiah." *Jewish Bible Quarterly* 40, no. 3 (2012): 159-162.

Saldarini, Anthony J. *Matthew's Christian-Jewish Community*. Chicago: The University of Chicago Press, 1994.

Sandmel, David Fox. "The Christian Reclamation of Judaism." Judaism 54, nos. 3/4 (2005) 251-262.

Schiffman, Lawrence H. *Qumran and Jerusalem*. Grand Rapids, MI: Eerdmans, 2010.

Schofield, Alison, and James C. Vanderkam. "Were the Hasmoneans Zadokites?" *Journal of Biblical Literature* 124, no.1 (2005): 73-87.

Scott, Jr., J. Julius. *Jewish Backgrounds of the New Testament*. Grand Rapids, MI: Baker, 1995.

Senior, Donald. "Viewing the Jewish Jesus of History through the Lens of Matthew's Gospel." In *Soundings in The Religion of Jesus: Perspectives and Methods in Jewish and Christian Scholarship*, eds. Bruce Chilton, Anthony Le Donne and Jacob Neusner, 81-95. Minneapolis, MN: Fortress, 2012.

Shapiro, Rami. *Ethics of the Sages*. Woodstock, VT: Skylight Paths, 2006.

Sigal, Phillip. *The Halakhah of Jesus of Nazareth according to the Gospel of Matthew*. Atlanta, GA: Society of Biblical Literature, 2007.

Silbiger, Steven. *The Jewish Phenomenon.* Lanham, NY: M. Evans, 2009.

Stassen, Glen H, and David P Gushee. *Kingdom Ethics.* Downers Grove, IL: Intervarsity, 2003.

Stern, David H. *Complete Jewish Bible.* Clarksville, TN: Jewish New Testament Publications, 1998.

_____. *Jewish New Testament Commentary.* Clarksville, TN: Jewish New Testament Publications, 1992.

Swartley, Willard. *Slavery, Sabbath, War & Women: case issues in biblical interpretation,* Scottdale, PA: Herald, 1983.

Talbert, Charles H. *Reading the Sermon on the Mount.* Columbia, SC: University of South Carolina Press, 2004.

Talmon, Shemaryahu. "Waiting for the Messiah: The Spiritual Universe of the Qumran Covenanters." In *Judaisms and their Messiahs,* eds. Jacob Neusner, William S. Green and Ernest Frerichs. Cambridge: Cambridge University Press, 1990.

Tamari, Meir. *Al Chet: Sins in the Market Place.* Brooklyn, NY: Judaica, 1996.

Taylor, Joan E. *The Essenes, the Scrolls, and the Dead Sea.* Oxford: Oxford University Press, 2012.

_____. *The Immerser.* Grand Rapids, MI: Eerdmans, 1997.

_____. "Review Article *Qumran in Context: Reassessing the Archaeological Evidence.*" *Bulletin of the Anglo-Israel Archaeological Society* 25, no. 1 (2007): 171-183.

Telushkin, Joseph. *A Code of Jewish Ethics.* New York: Bell Tower, 2009.

Toperoff, Shlomo. *Avot.* Northvale, NJ: Jason Aronson, 1997.

Touger, Eliyahu. *Maimonides Pirkei Avot.* New York: Moznaim, 1994.

Vermes, Geza. *Christian Beginnings From Nazareth to Nicaea, AD 30 - 325.* London: Penguin, 2012.

_____. "From Jewish to Gentile." *Biblical Archaeology Review* 38, no. 6 (2012): 53-58,78.

_____. *The Real Jesus.* London: SCM, 2009.

_____. *The Religion of Jesus the Jew.* London: SCM, 1993.

Vriezen, T. C., and A. S. van der Woude. *Ancient Israelite and Early Jewish Literature .* Leiden: Brill, 2005.

Walton, John H. *The Lost World of Genesis One: Ancient Cosmology and the Origins of Debate*. Downers Grove, IL: InterVarsity, 2009.

Waltzer, Michael. "War and Peace in the Jewish Tradition." In *The Ethics of War and Peace*, ed. Terry Nardin, 95-115. Princeton, NJ: Princeton University Press, 1996.

Weitzman, Steven. "Warring against Terror: The War Scroll and the Mobilization of Emotion." *Journal for the Study of Judaism*, 40, no. 2 (2009): 213-241.

Wenham, Gordon J. *Genesis 1-15*. vol. 1a. Word Biblical Commentary, Waco, TX: Word, 1987.

Wierzbicka, Anna. *What Did Jesus Mean? Explaining the Sermon on the Mount and the Parables in Simple and Universal Human Concepts*. Oxford: Oxford University Press, 2001.

Worth, Jr., Roland H. *The Sermon on the Mount: Its Old Testament Roots*. New York: Paulist, 1997.

Wright, N. T. *The New Testament and the People of God*. Minneapolis, MN: Fortress, 1992.

Wylen, Stephen M. *The Jews in the Time of Jesus*. New York: Paulist, 1996.

Young, Brad H. *Meet the Rabbis*. Peabody, MA: Hendrickson, 2007.